What others say...

"*Seeking and Savoring* is what Pamela Haddix's life has been about as long as I've known her. Authentic spiritual leadership is rare these days and Pam is just that—the real deal. This woman loves and walks with God. You will sense it in every one of the fifty-two chapters. Leaders worth taking seriously lead themselves well before they inflict themselves on those entrusted to their care. This self-leadership thing isn't easy. It demands consistent discipline. To do it well we need those who have gone before us to reach back and pull us forward. Through this devotional Pam helps us keep our walk with God present tense. Read each chapter slowly. Don't hurry through it. Listen for the voice of God as you read. If you do, you will emerge at the end of this devotional with a deeper heart of worship and an unforeseen life of joy."

—Dan Webster, Founder
Authentic Leadership, Inc.

"When does a spiritual lesson take perfect hold of you on your first exposure to it? 'Never,' is the appropriate answer. That is why *Seeking and Savoring* by Pamela Haddix gives so much help when it comes to the critical practice of daily personal worship. The daily devotions she's sculpted will *help you marinate in critical biblical insight* and will *guide you in spiritual practices* that will transform your personal daily worship from just 'having a quiet time' to interacting with the presence of the Lord Himself. Clear. Practical. Insightful. Inspiring. Fresh. All these dynamics and more will energize your daily times spent with the Lord. This book is important."

— Rev. Dr. Byron Spradlin, President
Artists in Christian Testimony Int'l.,

"Pam gets it. She knows Jesus. What a blessing she is. *Seeking and Savoring* really ministered to me and has changed how I spend time with Jesus. Because of this book, I now worship Him before I launch into any prayers or discussion. It just seems appropriate to do that because He is so worthy, and yet until I read *Seeking and Savoring*, it never occurred to me to do this. He's not there for us to dump our requests on. He already knows what they are anyway. He's a Person who deserves our undivided time and love, and Pam's book takes the reader to another realm of devotion to our glorious King. Thank you, Pam, for your obedience to write this wonderful book. I know many people will be blessed by this book, as I am."

— Kathy Curtis
www.christianbookformat.com

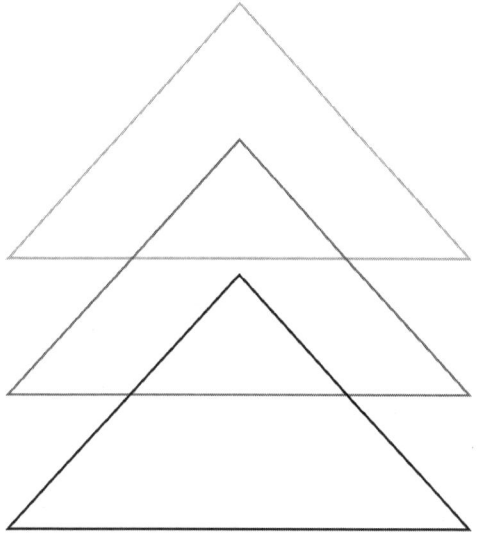

SEEKING
and *Savoring*

A Devotional to Encourage the Everyday Worship
of Our Extraordinary God

Pamela Haddix

Copyright © 2020 by Pamela Haddix

Seeking and Savoring
A Devotional to Encourage the Everyday Worship of Our Extraordinary God

By Pamela Haddix

Published by Earthwhile Publishing
Zeeland, Michigan

Published by DPZ Technology, LLC
Grand Rapids, Michigan

Printed in the United States of America

All rights reserved

Any reproduction of any of the contents of this book in any form without the proper permission is strictly prohibited.

ISBN: 978-1-939909-50-3

All rights reserved. No parts of this document may be reproduced or transmitted in any form, by any means (electronic, photocopying, recording, or otherwise) without the written permission of the author.

Unless otherwise noted, all Scripture is from the NEW AMERICAN STANDARD BIBLE, updated edition, Foundation Publications, Inc. Copyright © 1998 by the Lockman Foundation. All Rights Reserved.

Scripture quotations marked "ESV"® are from the Bible (The Holy Bible, English Standard Version®). Copyright © 2001 by Crossway Bibles, a publishing ministry of Good News Publishers. Used by permission. All rights reserved.

Scripture quotations marked "NIV" are from THE HOLY BIBLE, NEW INTERNATIONAL VERSION® NIV® Copyright © 1973, 1978, 1984 by International Bible Society® Used by permission. All rights reserved worldwide.

Scripture quotations marked "AKJV" are from The Authorized (King James) Version. Rights in the Authorized Version in the United Kingdom are vested in the Crown. Reproduced by permission of the Crown's patentee, Cambridge University Press.

Scripture quotations marked "BSB" are from The Holy Bible, Berean Study Bible, BSB. Copyright © 2016, 2018 by Bible Hub. Used by Permission. All Rights Reserved Worldwide.

Scripture quotations marked "ISV" are from the Holy Bible: International Standard Version® Release 2.0. Copyright © 1996-2013 by the ISV Foundation. Used by permission of Davidson Press, LLC. ALL RIGHTS RESERVED INTERNATIONALLY.

Scripture quotations marked "NKJV" are from the New King James Version. Copyright © 1982 by Thomas Nelson, Inc. Used by permission. All rights reserved.

Scripture quotations marked "CSB" are from the Christian Standard Bible® Copyright© 2017 by Holman Bible Publishers. Christian Standard Bible® and CSB® are federally registered trademarks of Holman Bible Publishers. Used by permission.

Cover Design: Kristeen VanderWall

This book is available at: pamelahaddix.com and amazon.com.

For...

... my incredible family — my amazing husband of forty years, John — whom I've served in ministry with since the beginning; our two incredible daughters and their husbands, Lindsy and Jordan, and Krista and Ben — who all love Jesus, their families, and others with all their might; and our seven grandchildren, Jude, Isaac, Owen, Naomi, Graham, Clara, and Miles — for being amazing, making me proud of who you are and growing to be everyday, and flat-out wrapping this Memaw around your little fingers. My heart is indeed full and I couldn't be more blessed by every single one of you. Our God is good and faithful.

And for anyone else out there who, like me, longs to seek and savor God more each day just as He deserves.

This is for you. And most of all, this is for Him. Let's allow Him to do His work in us — for His glory.

*"Ascribe to the Lord the glory due his name;
bring an offering and come before him!
Worship the Lord in the splendor of holiness;
tremble before him, all the earth;"*

1 Chronicles 16:29-30a

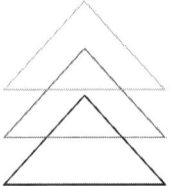

To learn more about Pamela Haddix, her ministry, or
how to order her books,
Seeking and Savoring or *Worship and the Word,* visit
pamelahaddix.com.

Contents

Before you begin xi

1. Who? 1
2. Struggle 5
3. Thankful 9
4. Know 13
5. Sin 17
6. Presence 21
7. Wonder-full 25
8. David (part 1) 28
9. David (part 2) 32
10. Grope 36
11. Stuck 39
12. Confidence 42
13. Lies 46
14. Surrender 50
15. Flourish 54
16. Everyday 57
17. Mary 61
18. Vision 65
19. Passivity 68
20. Drink 72
21. Grace 76
22. Remember 80
23. Breath 84

Seeking and Savoring

24. Silence 87
25. Battles 91
26. Paul 95
27. Talk 99
28. Give 102
29. Apathy 105
30. Near 109
31. Church (part 1) 113
32. Church (part 2) 117
33. Names 122
34. Jehoshaphat 126
35. Overwhelmed 131
36. Unreasonable 134
37. Adore 139
38. Stop 143
39. Flip 147
40. Snorkel? 150
41. Self 154
42. Leper 158
43. Wait 161
44. But 164
45. Reverence 169
46. Expect 173
47. Conversation 176
48. Broken 180
49. Cost 184
50. Shadrach (et al) 188
51. Listen 193
52. Him 197

Appendix
   Names, Titles, and Descriptions of God 201

Before you begin . . .

This book is for *me* as much as it is for anyone else. For I frequently find myself in a place of *re*learning (*you know what I mean?*) what God's will is for me as His worshiper as He's so beautifully laid out in His Word. Plus the battle against the enemy's attempts to make me feel like *I've got this all figured out* is ongoing. But I know from experience, there is great delight in fighting to be the worshiper God requires and deserves. I love how He rewards us with more of His presence, power, and glory!

The number one thing to know as we strive to grow to be a biblical worshiper is this—it needs to be about *Him*. Yes, *I'm* learning and *I'm* growing. But if I make it about *me* in the end (again, the enemy's twisted lie), it's not worship of *God*. My growth needs to be about *His glory*. Period.

One way I try to keep us on track is to include the beginnings of prayers at the end of each devotion. And I begin each one by thanking God and focusing on who He is before continuing with requests for ourselves. It's good to remember we need to *"Enter His gates with thanksgiving And His courts with praise. Give thanks to Him, bless His name"* (*Psalm 100:4*). It's also helpful to remember the way we were taught to begin prayer in Matthew

6:9: *"Our Father who is in heaven, Hallowed be Your name."* Let's keep it about *Him*.

Speaking of His name, I've included an appendix of the names, titles, and descriptions of God to help you to remember and focus on all He is in your worship of Him. I've found it helpful to keep it handy!

And while I've included a lot of Scripture in these devotions, I've also listed some that aren't written out. So, I highly encourage you to have your Bible handy so you can look up each passage in your own Bible, as well as go deep diving further in the additional ones I've listed. Let the *"living and active" (Hebrews 4:12)* Word of God be your guide—your teacher. (See what I did there?) I also encourage you to journal what God is teaching you so you can always look back to *remember*. If you read these devotions weekly, spend the entire week daily focusing on an emphasis God places on your heart from the devotion.

Finally, thank you for joining me on this journey of seeking and savoring God. It's a journey that will last for all eternity and never cease to delight and satisfy the soul. And most importantly, it will result in His greater glory.

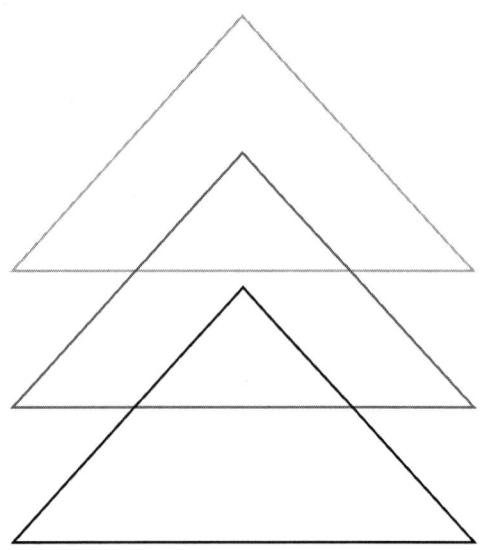

DAY ONE
Who?

I wonder if the disciples were perplexed, or even a little annoyed, when Jesus asked them this question: *"Who do **you** say that I am?" (Matthew 16:15).* Remember, they were the ones who had already committed to Jesus to the point of leaving everything to follow Him! Yet He *still* asked that crucial question of them.

When Peter answered, *"You are the Christ, the Son of the living God,"* Jesus responded with, *"Blessed are you, Simon Barjona, because flesh and blood did not reveal this to you, but My Father who is in heaven" (vv. 16-17).*

It is so important that we answer the same question often. No, daily! Because our honest answer absolutely affects everything else in our lives. It reflects not only *who* we believe God to be *intellectually*, but who we believe He is to us *personally*. And who we *really believe* God is can either blow the lid off of our worship life (in a great way) or utterly disintegrate it.

David understood his need to proclaim who God was in every situation. And the impact it had on his life and worship is obvious.

*"**The Lord is my shepherd**, I shall not want" (Psalm 23:1).*

"I said to the Lord, 'You are my Lord; I have no good besides You'" (Psalm 16:2).

"The Lord is my light and my salvation; Whom shall I fear? The Lord is the defense of my life: Whom shall I dread?" *(Psalm 27:1).*

"'I love You, O Lord, my strength.' ***The Lord is my rock and my fortress and my deliverer, My God, my rock,*** *in whom I take refuge;* ***My shield and the horn of my salvation, my stronghold.*** *I call upon the Lord, who is worthy to be praised, and I am saved from my enemies" (Psalm 18:1-3).*

"Every day I will bless You, And I will praise Your name forever and ever. ***Great is the Lord, and highly to be praised, And His greatness is unsearchable. . . The Lord is gracious and merciful; Slow to anger and great in lovingkindness"*** *(Psalm 145:2-3, 8).*

We could go on and on with just David, right? He knew there was power in *knowing* and *declaring* who God is! And remember, Jesus told Peter that His Father in heaven revealed the truth of who He was to Peter—that it wasn't something he could just pick up from *"flesh and blood."* So we need to make sure we spend enough time *seeking* and *listening* to our heavenly Father so *He* can reveal more of *Himself* to us. We can't rely just on the Sunday morning message or the latest podcast. Get with the Source! We can only grow in the true, experiential knowledge of God from His living Word and in His incredible presence.

Who?

And His presence? *Ahh*, it's where we discover that He *really is* all those things we sing about on Sunday! It's where the power behind the worship is birthed as the Holy Spirit is given the opportunity to speak, reveal, and guide us as we *diligently search* to know our *un*searchable God. And then, in His presence is where He *longs* to hear us pour out *all we know Him to be* in exaltation and adoration at His feet. What an amazing privilege He's given us!

So I want to make sure I *know* who He is. *Really* know. And let the experiential knowledge of God change my life and empower my worship. I want to *know*, and I want to tell Him *often*. He asks us,

> *Who do you say that I am? Today. In that place you're in. Who do you believe I am for you right here – right now?*

David replied, "O God, **You are my God**; I shall seek You earnestly" (Psalm 63:1).

Reflect

Who do I say that He is — right here, right now, right where I am today? What can I do to continually grow in my experiential knowledge of God? Observing David, how would experiential knowledge of God fuel my worship?

Respond

Lord God, thank You for revealing Yourself to me through Your Word. I praise You for being my Shepherd, my Light, and my Salvation — my Strength, my Rock, and Deliverer. I praise You for Your grace and mercy that You pour out for me every single day. Open my heart and mind to see and understand all of who You are. I invite You to guide and empower my worship as I seek Your face. . . . <continue>

DAY TWO
Struggle

I'm really not oblivious to the very real struggle worship can be. Beyond hearing many friends express their own frustrations with their worship lives, I remember! I've been there! And frankly, I *still* fight to stay out of the slippery pit of status quo, *it's-just-what-we-do* worship.

And that should be good news for you! Why? Because that means that *I'm living proof that you can get out of that pit*. I'm living proof that *the patience of God extends into our worship life*. His love never stops drawing us and compelling us. His patience and grace extend way into our seeking Him and our worship of Him.

He longs for us to lift our eyes *off* of ourselves and all of the distractions (that range from important to worthless) and *fix our eyes and heart on Him* (Psalm 57:7). And when we finally stop and *really* look—take in *all* He wants to show us of Himself—we *can't help* but humbly respond in *worship*.

But the enemy wants us to think one of many lies:

- God would never notice *my* worship.
- It's too much work.
- My slight effort really is *enough*.
- I should wait until I *feel* like it.

Seeking and Savoring

- He already knows how I feel.
- It's really *not* a big deal anyway.

Either way, we decide we might as well settle for disconnected, half-hearted, routine worship—or give up all together. Well, that's what the enemy is counting on! Think about it—those arguments put the focus on *me*. And as long as I'm looking at *me*, I'm going to struggle.

Remember, *"the **kindness** of God leads you to repentance"* (Romans 2:4). And *"I, by **Your great love**, can come into Your house; in reverence I bow down toward Your holy temple"* (Psalm 5:7, NIV).

It's His *kindness* and *love* that draw us into a relationship with Him and ultimately to pure worship. It's the *same love* that offered His Son, Jesus, to die on the cross for our sins so we might have access to Him *by grace through faith* (Ephesians 2:8). And the *same love* gives us His Spirit so He can fill us with every spiritual blessing and guide us to His throne.

The absolute *power* for worship is available the moment we turn our focus on *Him*. *He's* the purpose. *He's* the goal. *He's* the only worthy recipient of our undivided attention—*and* the motivation to finally have a *holy dissatisfaction* with status quo worship!

Seeing Him makes us *not want to give up* just because it's a battle—and *not want to settle* instead of vigorously pursuing. *Seeing Him* makes us want to *respond* with unbridled worship!

Yes, He *commands* us to worship Him.

"YOU SHALL WORSHIP THE LORD YOUR GOD, AND SERVE HIM ONLY" (Matthew 4:10).

But that command comes from our Creator *lovingly and persistently drawing us so we might fulfill what He created us to do. Worship* Him. It's a breathtaking privilege far beyond a mere obligation.

So, *pursue* Him — to intimately *know* and *love* Him. Pursue His guidance in your worship. Enter worship having prayed for a surrendered heart and mind focused purely on Him and for strength to fight the enemy's darts. It's worth the fight! God understands the battle and His Spirit can empower you to conquer it.

If you're at home, set an alarm if you need to be somewhere or do something afterward — so you're not clock-watching and can singularly focus. Arm yourself with truth from His Word about *who He is* and His call to worship Him. *Do whatever it takes* to have that vertical, intimate communion with the heart of God as you pour out your response to all He is in worship.

And even though worship is not about *me* at all, *still, "He is a rewarder of those who seek Him" (Hebrews 11:6).* And the rewards of our God's transforming presence and the greater glimpse of His glory are beyond compare.

Don't settle. Join me in the battle. Let's worship our incredible God!

"My heart is fixed, O God, my heart is fixed; I will sing and give praise" (Psalm 57:7, AKJV).

Seeking and Savoring

Reflect

How do I personally relate to the struggle that we all face as worshipers of God? What can I do to fight that battle head-on? What steps should I take to pursue God more?

Respond

Lord God, thank You that Your patience extends even into my worship life. Thank You for always drawing me to Yourself. I praise You for Your love and kindness that never wavers but pursues me. Strengthen my resolve to have a surrendered heart and mind focused on seeking and worshiping You. Help me to not settle for less. . . .
<continue>

DAY THREE
Thankful

I was reminded recently of how dependent my *worship* life is on the condition of my *thankful* (or not) heart when I read this verse:

> *"Through Him then, let us continually offer up a **sacrifice of praise** to God, that is, **the fruit of lips that give thanks to His name**" (Hebrews 13:15).*

There are several ingredients in having a true worshiper's heart, and the Bible says an important one is *thankfulness*. Worship is the *fruit* of our *thankfulness* to God — it requires a thankful heart. In fact, we must . . .

> *"**Enter His gates with thanksgiving** and* [then] *His courts with praise. Give thanks to Him, bless His name. For the* LORD *is good; His lovingkindness is everlasting and His faithfulness to all generations" (Psalm 100:4-5).*

You have to go through the gate to get to the courts. I believe that we sometimes miss out on intimacy with God in His courts, simply because we're not thankful enough to get through the gate. It's important to God. We need to approach His throne remembering and being thankful for His goodness, His lovingkindness, and His faithfulness.

Seeking and Savoring

We get the same encouragement from Psalm 95:2- 3a:

> *"Let us come before His presence with thanksgiving, let us shout joyfully to Him with psalms. For the* Lord *is a great God . . . "*

I believe this is important because a thankful heart recognizes the *relationship* between the blessings of this earthly existence and the *incredible goodness of God*. A thankful heart is aware of *God's power* at work when life's limitations don't rule the moment. A thankful heart acknowledges God is *still who He says He is* even when things don't go the way I hoped. And a thankful heart knows *none* of this is about *me*, but *Him*.

Every time we stop to give thanks to God—to acknowledge His hand at work in, through, and around us—it fertilizes the soil that worship grows in. And it makes the *worship-filled "fruit"* of those *"lips that give thanks"* more lavish and abundant. God is glorified!

Here's more encouragement:

> *"He who offers a* **sacrifice of thanksgiving** *honors Me" (Psalm 50:23).*

> *"O* Lord*, You are my God; I will exalt You, I will* **give thanks** *to Your name; For You have worked wonders, Plans formed long ago, with perfect faithfulness" (Isaiah 25:1).*

> *"Praise the* Lord*! I will* **give thanks** *to the* Lord *with all my heart, In the company of the upright and in the assembly" (Psalm 111:1).*

Thankful

To neglect to show God the gratitude due Him— even offering a flippant *thanks*—is being *un*thankful. *Un*grateful. *Un*appreciative. And shows *no real understanding* of *who God is*. It's like saying, *I deserved this. I earned this. I made this happen.* Or even subconsciously – *I don't need God.*

> *"For even though they **knew** God, they **did not honor Him as God or give thanks**, but they became futile in their speculations, and their **foolish heart** was darkened" (Romans 1:21).*

Would you join me in this simple prayer for a thankful heart?

Lord God, You are holy, mighty, and faithful to all generations. You are above all, yet Your love never fails. Your mercy never ends. And for all of these things and more, I thank You. Forgive me for all the times I haven't been truly thankful – when I haven't acknowledged Your hand, Your goodness, Your faithfulness, or Your blessings that go WAY beyond what I deserve. You have given me eternity with You – and if that were the only benefit of salvation, that would be an unearned, undeserved, lavish gift. But You pour out MORE Every. Single. Day – Your presence, Your power, Your help, Your guidance, Your love, Your empowering gifts, Your grace (oh, Your grace!) in times good and hard, and more! How can I NOT be thankful? May I never take a moment of this life with You for granted – not a single breath of air, not a beat of my heart, not each new day, not any opportunity to sing Your praise. I am thankful. May my heart never be foolish, but stay set on, humbled before, and thankful to YOU. May I always worship You as you deserve. In Jesus' holy name. Amen.

Reflect

Does expressing my thankfulness to God come easily to me, or is it a struggle? How do I need to grow in my thankfulness to God? How should I incorporate it into my worship of Him?

Respond

<continue from the prayer above as you feel led>

DAY FOUR
Know

Knowing the person of God is crucial for true worship to happen. It's essential. It's foundational. For without it our worship would be like a choir without a song to sing. In Hosea 6:6, we read,

> *"For I delight in loyalty rather than sacrifice, and in **knowledge of God** rather than burnt offerings."*

In Jesus' priestly prayer He said, *"And this is eternal life, that they may **know You**, the only true God, and Jesus Christ whom You have sent" (John 17:3).*

These verses elevate the knowledge of God to extreme importance. In fact, the Hebrew word *da'at*, translated as *"knowledge of God"* in Hosea 6:6, most accurately expresses an *experiential* knowledge. It's way beyond the mere acknowledgment that God simply exists, for even the demons acknowledge that (James 2:19). But it expresses a personal, intimate awareness of who God is and what He's done that results in an awe-inspired, complete, and utter devotion to Him.

If we could pray but one prayer, it should be that we would grow to know and love God more. When those two things are happening, all other aspects of the Christian life—such as prayer, obedience, serving, and giving—grow as a direct result. And that includes our

Seeking and Savoring

worship life. True worship is grounded in the critical issue of knowing and loving God.

Here's the problem. There's a tendency to view God in human terms, as actually being no different from ourselves. Now no one will quickly agree that they do that. But how often do we consent with the voice in our head that whispers, *God can't (or wouldn't) do that* or *He doesn't really care (or listen)*? That list of doubts could go on and on. We sing the great songs, mouth the verses, and nod in agreement. But when it comes down to what we really, deeply believe, so many of us have little ambition to want to get to know, or especially bow in worship to, *that* God. In Psalm 50:21, God confronted those who didn't honor Him with, *"You thought that I was just like you."* So the question needs to be asked: Are we worshiping the God of the Bible who is *infinite* and *holy*—or a god that's limited by what our minds can grasp and our society can accept?

Psalm 145:3 says, *"Great is the LORD, and highly to be praised; And His greatness is unsearchable."*

And in Romans 11:33, 36 we read, *"Oh, the depth of the riches both of the wisdom and knowledge of God! How unsearchable are His judgments and unfathomable His ways! ... For from Him and through Him and to Him are all things. To Him be the glory forever. Amen."*

According to these verses, praise and glory belong to the unsearchable, unfathomable God! None of us will ever understand God perfectly on this side of heaven, for He cannot be limited by any kind of human definition. But we get into trouble when we try to make God

Know

too much like what we know and don't try to grow in the true knowledge of Him.

We're obviously not talking about mere head knowledge. We need to continually ask God to help us see Him more clearly and more fully; and we need to respond by pursuing a greater intimacy with the God who's revealing Himself to us. We do that by spending priority time with Him in the Word and in prayer. Only then will our relationship and heart knowledge of Him grow.*

Only then will our worship of God deepen and grow.

Reflect
Do I feel my worship stifled by my limited view of God? How would increasing my knowledge of God affect my worship life? How do I feel God leading me to grow in my knowledge of Him and my depths of worship of Him? What steps should I take to do that?

Seeking and Savoring

Respond

My God, thank You for desiring an intimate relationship with me. I praise You for being the unsearchable, unfathomable God, yet You long to reveal Yourself to me. Help me to see You more clearly and fully. And help me to know how to best respond to what You reveal of Yourself to me. I invite Your Spirit to prod me when I'm slacking and to guide me in a deeper heart knowledge of You. . . . <continue>

*This devotion includes excerpts from my book, *Worship and the Word*.

DAY FIVE
Sin

Worship is not an event or practice that can be separated in the least from the rest of a person's life. In other words, if we choose to live a life that is contrary to God's Word, then any words of worship we may mouth at church, or anywhere else, fall empty. That's because sin draws us away from God and away from true worship. But He hasn't left us in this hopeless situation. We have a choice.

Hebrews 10:19, 22 gives rich insight into what kind of preparation God expects from His worshipers:

> *"Therefore, brethren, since we have confidence to enter the holy place by the blood of Jesus . . . [Then] Let us draw near with a sincere heart in full assurance of faith, having our hearts sprinkled clean from an evil conscience and our bodies washed with pure water."*

Here's a verse that gives us four conditions necessary to be ready to *"enter the holy place"* or a place of worship. The first is having a *"sincere heart."* We need to have hearts that are truly fixed on God, not self-absorbed, hypocritical, preoccupied, or apathetic. Second, we need to draw near *"in full assurance of faith."* The worshiper needs to come to God fully assured that his access is by faith alone in Jesus Christ. The third condition listed here is *"having hearts sprinkled clean."* We must come knowing that we only have the right to be there because we've been cleansed by the blood of Jesus. And finally, we come with *"our bodies washed with pure water."* I believe this refers to the necessary daily confession of sin—just as 1 John 1:9 refers to God's faithfulness to *"cleanse us from all unrighteousness"* as we confess our sin. If we fulfill these four conditions, we will have every *"confidence"* to enter His presence and worship.

So what if you desire to *"enter the holy place"* to worship, and upon coming, realize that you don't have clean hands or a pure, sincere heart? The first step is to agree with God about the sin that He's showing you. Call the sin what it is and repent, which involves a change in attitude and action. Sincerely pray and ask God to forgive and cleanse you of the sin, thank Him for His promised forgiveness (1 John 1:9), and ask Him to empower you through His Spirit to walk in a way pleasing to Him. True worship involves a surrender and submission of everything we are before God.

This all leads us to ask: Are too few experiencing the kind of worship that God intended? Absolutely. So is this an insurmountable barrier? Absolutely NOT! True worship, just like the victorious Christian life, is the fruit of daily seeking to live in the power of the Holy Spirit. Just as we received Christ by faith, faith is the only means by which we can live the Spirit-filled life. It's not something that God ever intended that we do on our own. There is an unlimited supply of grace and power to live the Christian life available to us at all times! Even though it's the enemy's greatest desire to defeat us every step of the way, our God is a God of incredible grace!

Sin

I don't want to neglect to mention how we are even allowed to enter the holy presence of the Lord God Almighty to begin with. *"But as for me, by Your abundant lovingkindness I will enter Your house, At Your holy temple I will bow in reverence for You" (Psalm 5:7)*. It's only out of His *"abundant lovingkindness"* that we're ushered into His presence. He longs for us to be there. It was out of His abundant love that He offered His Son, Jesus, to die on the cross for our sins, so that we might have access to Him by grace through faith (Ephesians 2:8).

His love draws us. His love allows us. His love fills us. It's out of His undeserved love and grace that we have anything to offer back to Him in worship. And it's out of this love that He yearns for us to be His intimate worshipers. There's no greater goal!

Reflect

Do I remember a time of feeling unable to worship God due to unconfessed sin in my life? Do I regularly experience confidence entering my time of worship? How does the truth of God's love drawing us to worship affect how I view it? How is God leading me to respond to the truths shared in the verses here?

Seeking and Savoring

Respond

Lord God, thank You for the blood of Jesus that makes it possible for me to confidently come into Your presence. Thank You for Your faithfulness and mercy that forgives my sin and makes me clean. I praise You for Your abundant love that continually draws me and fills me instead of leaving me in a place of defeat. Help me to not live a life contrary to Your Word. . . . <continue>

*This devotion includes excerpts from my book, *Worship and the Word*.

DAY SIX
Presence

What would you say if I told you **God wants us to *expect* to engage with Him closely as we worship?** Second Chronicles 15:2 says, " . . . *the* LORD *is with you when you are with Him. And if you seek Him, He will let you find Him."* The Bible reveals a God who is constantly inviting us into His presence!

He *wants* to be seen by His children. He *longs* for us to know Him intimately. He knows that as we enter His presence in worship, each glimpse of His glory and every moment of awesome revelation wins a bigger piece of our hearts. And He knows our passion to come back for more grows as our picture of Him grows. Because there is *so much more* to our God than we could ever imagine!

And the most humbling discovery is that the God who created the heavens and the earth actually does love us deeply and longs to encounter us closely. We shouldn't ever cease to be amazed at those overwhelming truths. The Word's call to us is simple: *"Draw near to God and He will draw near to you"* (James 4:8a).

Yet how many of us enter our times of worship expecting nothing of the sort from God? Maybe He feels far away, or maybe the mystery is just too great, and we honestly *do* doubt His presence. Yet, the reason we don't have to go to the temple to worship anymore, as in Old Testament times, is because we *each* are now a temple! As 1 Corinthians 3:16 says, *"Do you not know that you are a temple of God and that the Spirit of God dwells in you?"*

So you and I are living, breathing, skin-clad temples! And we can *expect* intimacy in worship with the God who lives in us. These are the moments that He truly longs for—when we turn and engage with Him with all our being. He's already right there waiting—we don't have to worship God from a distance!

Listen to David in this psalm:

> *"O God, You are my God; I shall seek You earnestly; My soul thirsts for You, my flesh yearns for You, In a dry and weary land where there is no water. Thus* **I have seen You in the sanctuary***, To see Your power and Your glory. Because Your lovingkindness is better than life, My lips will praise You. So I will bless You as long as I live; I will lift up my hands in Your name. My soul is satisfied as with marrow and fatness, And my mouth offers praises with joyful lips"* (Psalm 63:1-5).

David *sought* and *expected* God's presence in his worship. He recognized God's glory and movement in his life in marvelous ways as His presence changed David's very life!

> *"How blessed is the one whom You choose and* **bring near to You***, To dwell in Your courts. We will be satisfied with the goodness of Your house, Your holy temple"* (Psalm 65:4).

Presence

There are no words that can express the depth of God's desire for us to experience His presence, any more than they can express the depths of God Himself.

I just know that the God who sings and dances over us must *relish* those moments when we stop to pour out our praise and adoration—straining along the way to get past the world so we can catch a greater glimpse of His glory.

I'm not talking about working up a bunch of feelings, though they will come at times more strongly than others. I'm talking about *seeking and responding rightly to the truth of who God is* in that place where He's waiting to *commune* with us and *reveal* a little more of Himself each time.

The thought of it leaves me speechless.

But He is faithful. He is gracious. And He will honor those who seek to be His worshipers with a clearer picture of Himself and greater taste of His presence. There is no greater privilege in this life!

"*O taste and see that the* LORD *is good*" *(Psalm 34:8).*

Seeking and Savoring

Reflect

How does that make me feel to know that God wants me to *expect* to engage with Him closely as I worship? How does that impact my personal worship life? Which of these verses do I feel God wants me to claim over my worship?

Respond

My God, I thank You for the promise of Your presence. Thank You for longing to bring me near to You. I praise You for Your power and glory that You reveal to me as I draw near to Your throne. And I praise You for Your faithfulness and grace toward me. Help me to stop often to engage You and pour out all I am at Your feet. . . . .
<continue>

*This devotion includes excerpts from my book, *Worship and the Word*.

DAY SEVEN
Wonder-full

The much-anticipated day had *finally* come. I got the text from my spy, "She just went back." And then, "It's close!" I felt my heart noticeably start pounding harder and faster in expectancy.

I grabbed my earbuds as I was suddenly compelled to listen to Bethel Music's song, "Wonder." *"May we never lose our wonder . . ."* And I would've let the tears welling up in my eyes turn into a flood were it not for the three-year-old next to me on the couch (who was telling the animated crayons on TV what needed to be colored — "The pumpkin! The pumpkin's orange!"). This oldest grandchild of mine (and son of our oldest daughter, Lindsy, aka, the spy) had never seen his Memaw lose control before, so I didn't think now was a good time to start. But *our* baby girl, Krista, giving birth to her *first two babies* at the same time, was uncharted territory for me. And *so much* about it was overwhelming right then.

Not the least of which was a wonder for my marvelous God and what He was doing and revealing in that moment: Answer to prayer. Redemption of more difficult times. New life. No, new *lives*! And above all, a picture of His hand . . . His mercy . . . His grace . . . His love . . . His beauty . . . and His blessings.

Seeking and Savoring

And then God reminded me. *I'm this breathtakingly wonder-full all the time.*

All the time. He's wonderful in those moments that are overwhelmingly *difficult*, as well as the ones like this that are overwhelmingly *amazing*. When everything's going as planned, and when I slump into the mundane and struggle to find anything remotely incredible at all, God is *wonder-full*.

He's always working and moving, redeeming and creating. At all times He's totally and completely, *oh, so wonderful*. He can't be anything else! I *need* to remember that, and I need to *respond* to that truth by worshiping Him. Because I *lose* my wonder when I stop seeking. Stop gazing. Stop remembering. Stop striving to know more of *who He is*. It doesn't make Him *less* wonderful — it just makes my sight and soul dulled to His wonder. It just makes me fail to see His glory, so I *fail* to *glorify* Him.

For our sweet, tiny Clara Jane and Graham Odell, everything was suddenly new. *Everything.* But you know what? My God is in the business of *new* every day! He *delights* in new! I just need to look for it and stand in awe and wonder!

"The Lord's *lovingkindnesses indeed never cease, For His compassions never fail. They are **new** every morning; Great is Your faithfulness" (Lamentations 3:22-23).*

"Look among the nations! Observe! Be astonished! **Wonder!** *Because I am doing something in your days — You would not believe if you were told" (Habakkuk 1:5).*

*"Many, O LORD my God, are the **wonders** which You have done"* (Psalm 40:5).

Can you hear the gasps? The *"Ahhhh!"* ringing out from these verses?

Because, I know they're even greater than our response to the tiny wonders He had for us in the hospital that day. Because we worship a wonder-full God!

Reflect

What wonders can I list right now about God that have moved me personally? Do I need to spend more time fueling my soul with the wonder of God? What steps should I take so I don't stop striving to know Him more fully — don't stop to be in wonder of Him?

Respond

*God, I praise You for being overwhelmingly full of incredible wonder. There are wonders of Your love, Your compassion, and Your faithfulness towards me. Help me to stop to be fascinated by Your beauty. Help me to never stop striving to **see** You — seeking to **know** You — growing to **love** You. Open my eyes so I never lose the wonder of who You are and what You're doing around me. At all times. Because You alone are God. . . .* <continue>

DAY EIGHT
David
(part 1)

There is so much we could learn from David about how He *seeks* and *savors* God in worship. Let's dig in to see what his prolific, soul-baring psalms reveal to us about how we can worship with a heart like his.

1) David's psalms show how hard he sought to know God.

> *"The heavens declare the glory of God; the skies proclaim the work of His hands. Day after day they pour forth speech; night after night they reveal knowledge. . . . The law of the Lord is perfect, refreshing the soul. The statutes of the Lord are trustworthy, making wise the simple. The precepts of the Lord are right, giving joy to the heart. The commands of the Lord are radiant, giving light to the eyes. The fear of the Lord is pure, enduring forever. The decrees of the Lord are firm, and all of them are righteous"* (Psalm 19:1-2, 7-9, BSB).

We all know that God called David *"a man after My heart"* (Acts 13:22). And he displays that all over the psalms. Here in Psalm 19, after poetically seeing God in the intricacies of the heavens, he immediately expresses his love of God's law. I love this picture of how David *seeks,* sees, and is in *awe* of God. The same God who created the breathtaking works around us is the same God who spoke the Word and still speaks it into our lives. Those are all reasons to worship Him.

2) David fully engaged his heart in worship to God.

> *"O God, You are my God; I shall seek You earnestly; My soul thirsts for You, my flesh yearns for You, In a dry and weary land where there is no water. Thus I have seen You in the sanctuary, To see Your power and Your glory. Because Your lovingkindness is better than life, My lips will praise You. So I will bless You as long as I live; I will lift up my hands in Your name. My soul is satisfied as with marrow and fatness, And my mouth offers praises with joyful lips" (Psalm 63:1-5).*

This is the response of David's *heart* towards God at a very difficult time in his life. (And he had plenty of those!) God isn't just some mighty but distant God to David. God is *his* God, and David *adored* Him. Oh, how we should each pray that our hearts would be open and free to respond to our loving God with adoring worship!

3) David didn't take approaching God's throne lightly.

> *"O LORD, who may abide in Your tent? Who may dwell on Your holy hill? He who walks with integrity, and works righteousness, And speaks truth in his heart" (Psalm 15:1-2).*

David wanted his worship to be acceptable to God and knew it couldn't be separated in the least from the rest of his life. He knew if he chose to live a life contrary to God's word, then any words of worship he may utter would fall empty (Mark 7:6-7a).

4) David embraced the sacrifice of worship.

> *"Willingly I will sacrifice to You; I will give thanks to Your name, O LORD, for it is good"* (Psalm 54:6).

David knew that any *"sacrifice"* of his time, energy, or focus in worship paled greatly to the glimpse of God's greatness and goodness. The *"willing"* sacrifice is a heartfelt expression of an intimate relationship with the God who rescued him from his pit and drew him, awestruck and humbled, to his knees. It's the result of passionately pursuing the Lord God Almighty who *first* passionately pursued him—and *us!*

5) David responded when his worship revealed sin.

> *"To you, O LORD, I lift up my soul. . . . Lead me in Your truth and teach me, For You are the God of my salvation; For You I wait all the day. . . . All the paths of the LORD are lovingkindness and truth To those who keep His covenant and His testimonies. For Your name's sake, O LORD, Pardon my iniquity, for it is great"* (Psalm 25:1, 5, 10-11).

While remembering the goodness and faithfulness of his God in worship, David was sometimes led into a time of confession. He learned that an immediate, contrite response at the prompting of the Holy Spirit would be met with not only embracing forgiveness, but also with invigorated intimacy in worship.

David (part 1)

We'll continue exploring David's psalms in our next devotion, but take the time to reflect and respond to what God's revealing so far.

Reflect

What do I appreciate most about David's example as a worshiper so far? What do I think I should personally learn and apply from David's worship? What steps could I take to do that?

Respond

Dear God, thank You for the incredible picture of worship I get from David. I praise You for Your incredible love and grace that gives me the humble privilege to come before You. Teach me to fully engage my heart and respond to You completely as I come to worship You.... <continue>

DAY NINE
David
(part 2)

Digging into these incredible psalms of David's is like finding worship gold. Excavating a little more, here are some more ways we can worship with a heart like David's.

6) David learned to worship God in any situation.

> *"O God, You are my God; I shall seek You earnestly; My soul thirsts for You, my flesh yearns for You, In a dry and weary land where there is no water. Thus I have seen You in the sanctuary, To see Your power and Your glory. Because Your lovingkindness is better than life, My lips will praise You"* (Psalm 63:1-3).

David wrote Psalm 63 when he was in the wilderness of Judah, probably after he fled Jerusalem at the time of Absalom's rebellion (2 Samuel 15). Obviously, the place David is in at this point in his life isn't all that great. God was protecting him, but He hadn't changed his situation yet. David's *"life"* was on the line, and he wasn't in denial about that. Instead, He was living in the midst of the reality of *who God was for him* in that situation. And it led him to worship.

David (part 2)

7) David's honesty with God drew him into worship.

"How long, O LORD? Will You forget me forever? How long will You hide Your face from me? How long shall I take counsel in my soul, Having sorrow in my heart all the day? How long will my enemy be exalted over me? ... But I have trusted in Your lovingkindness; My heart shall rejoice in Your salvation. I will sing to the LORD, Because He has dealt bountifully with me" (Psalm 13:1-2, 5-6).

Speaking of *any* situation—David knew that God could handle the expression of his painful emotions and that it would lead him to the *truth*. *And* to worship. *God loves me. God is my salvation. God has dealt bountifully with me.*

8) David expected his perspective to be changed during worship.

"When I consider Your heavens, the work of Your fingers, the moon and the stars, which you have ordained; What is man that You should take thought of him, and the son of man that You should care for him?" (Psalm 8:3-4).

As David beheld the indescribable glory of the Lord, he was struck by his own utter unworthiness in comparison. It was clearly a "You are God, and I am not" moment. We all need more of those.

9) David allowed his worship to usher him into prayer.

"You, Lord, are good, and ready to forgive, and abundant in lovingkindness to all who call upon You. Give

Seeking and Savoring

ear, O LORD, to my prayer; And give heed to the voice of my supplications!" (Psalm 86:5-6).

As David entered prayer during a time of great distress in Psalm 86, he wisely used it as a time to focus on God and worship. And as he put his *need* in perspective with *who God is,* the Holy Spirit prompted him to pray.

Our *single focus* in worship needs to be on our glorious God and not on our long list of requests. However, we need to be quick, like David, any time the Holy Spirit prompts us to respond to the God we're exalting with a revealed need.

10) David was fully surrendered in his worship response to God.

"And so it was, that when the bearers of the ark of the LORD had gone six paces, he sacrificed an ox and a fatling. And David was dancing before the LORD with all his might" (2 Samuel 6:13-14).

When David was invaded by the knowledge and love of God, then his natural resulting worship was a bit more demonstrative than casual, distant viewers of God. For God is not a casual God! And David's dancing was a beautiful act of worship to Him. (If you read a little further in 2 Samuel, not everyone thought so!)

I'm glad David was so *prolific,* and *poetic,* and *real*—aren't you? It makes it so much easier to see and fall in love with our God!

David (part 2)

This is obviously not an exhaustive list of things we could learn from David's worship. (He's given us a lot to study!) But it's enough to encourage us to worship with a heart like his that says, *"My heart is steadfast, O God, my heart is steadfast; I will sing, yes, I will sing praises!"* (Psalm 57:7).

Reflect

What do I appreciate most about David's example as a worshiper in these psalms? What do I think I should personally learn and apply from David's worship overall? What steps do I feel led to take to do that?

Respond

Dear God, thank You for giving David an incredible worshiper's heart for me to learn from. I praise You that You still long to commune with me as I worship so I might gain a bigger picture of Yourself. Help me to come with a sincere, surrendered heart — expecting your movement in my life as I bask in Your presence. May worshiping You be a great priority and sustaining force in my life at all times. . . . <continue>

DAY TEN
Grope

I've always been a vivid dreamer. And apparently having a baby kicked that into high gear!

Not long after the birth of our first daughter, I began having a crazy, repetitive dream. During my already-sleep-deprived night, I would dream I had fallen asleep while nursing my baby girl and *dropped* her. (Can you moms relate?) And the dream was so intense, my husband, John, would find me on my hands and knees on the floor groping in the darkness calling out, "Lindsy . . . Lindsy . . . ," as if she would answer. He would sleepily say from the bed, "Honey, Lindsy's fine. She's in her crib. Come back to bed." But seriously, how in the world would he know that? I was the one who fed and dropped her! The dream was so vivid, John would often have to get out of bed to get me up out of my groping position on the floor to help me back into bed. And sometimes I would have to go into the nursery to confirm my baby girl's whereabouts. I can't tell you *how many times* I actually did this!

I was reminded of these crazy dreams recently when I read Paul's sermon on Mars Hill where he said,

> "*And He made from one man every nation of mankind to live on all the face of the earth, . . . that they would*

Grope

seek God, if perhaps they might grope for Him and find Him, though He is not far from each one of us; for in Him we live and move and exist" (Acts 17:26-28a).

I feel like Paul at first said we should *"seek God"* and then decided to kick it up a notch and said, "No, *grope for Him!"* And when I stop to think about what groping for God might look like, I wonder if He sees me passionately grope for Him like I did for my baby girl in the night.

Whether it's in those moments that are so dark, I can't see my hand in front of my face, or there's so much clutter, my view is blocked. Or maybe it's just remembering from His Word that there's *so much more* to be found — *do I get on my hands and knees and grope for God until I find Him?* The verse in Acts says He's *"not far"*!

We need to grope *"to comprehend with all the saints what is the breadth and length and height and depth, and to know the love of Christ which surpasses knowledge, that you may be filled up to all the fullness of God"* (Ephesians 3:18-19). Even though *"His greatness is unsearchable"* (Psalm 145:3), He still tells us *"You will seek Me and **find** Me when you search for Me with all your heart"* (Jeremiah 29:13).

So how much do we miss out on when we don't *grope* for God? What is He longing to show us *if we'll just get on our hands and knees and go after Him?* What dimensions will that add to our *worship* when we delve into those greater depths of God?

"He made" each and every one of us *"that [we] would seek God, if perhaps [we] might grope for Him and find Him."*

Seeking and Savoring

Because we're all hands-and-knees desperate.

That is very much a part of how He longs for us to *"live and move and exist"* and *"be filled up to all the fullness of God."*

Let's not just *read* about God. Let's not just pray *casual* prayers and say *passive* words of worship to Him. Let's invite Him to show us how to literally *grope for the greater depths of who He is*. He promises to be found! And then let's *respond* in worship.

Reflect

Why do I think it's so hard to realize each of us are hands-and-knees desperate for God? Do I take the time and energy to grope for God? How? And how is God leading me to respond to these verses?

Respond

Lord God, I thank You and praise You that You're not far. I thank You that You long for me to comprehend the depths of Your love for me so You might fill me up. I praise You for that overwhelming love and goodness and faithfulness that never stop drawing me closer to You. Help me to realize my desperate need to grope for You, and be faithful to follow through every day. . . . <continue>

DAY ELEVEN
Stuck

We *love* God. We *love* learning from His Word to us, the Bible. We confess sin as the Holy Spirit reveals it so we can walk closely with Him. And we *love* singing all the great songs about our Savior. In fact, the worship time is one of our favorite parts of our church service. Right? So what are we missing?

There are so many places we can get stuck on this Christian journey to become worshipers of our great God. Even for those of us who strive to seek after God — in the daily reading of His Word and prayer — there's a common place of stuck-ness when it comes to worship that I frequently hear about. Okay, that *I've been stuck in!*

I think our *focus* often gets stuck. We get stuck at *merely* seeing, believing, and proclaiming.

What? But those are great things! Absolutely, they are! And necessary! But when it comes to worship, God wants us to move *beyond* seeing, believing, and proclaiming to *responding*. He wants us to get beyond standing outside the temple telling everyone how wonderful our God is, to entering the holy place, intimately bowing at the foot of His throne, and pouring out all we are in submissive response to the God who's revealing Himself to us there.

It's a dialing in of our *focus* and *attention*, so our hearts and minds can *respond* in humble adoration. It's looking Him in the face and saying, "*You* are *my* God. *You* are holy. *You* are worthy. I offer *all I am* to You." And then, seeing Him standing there with His arms open wide inviting you into His presence: *Welcome, My child — I've been waiting for you. I love it when you come here. I receive your offering and pour out more of My glory for you to see. Please come often. I have so much for you here.*

We can sing songs as enthusiastically as the next guy. But until our hearts choose that vertical, intimate communion with the heart of the God we're singing about, it's not worship. Worship is an offering *to* Him, not just words *about* Him.

I love how undivided David's heart was in pouring out his adoration to God:

> *"O God, You are my God; I shall seek You earnestly; My soul thirsts for You, my flesh yearns for You, In a dry and weary land where there is no water. Thus I have seen You in the sanctuary, To see Your power and Your glory. Because Your lovingkindness is better than life, My lips will praise You. So I will bless You as long as I live; I will lift up my hands in Your name. My soul is satisfied as with marrow and fatness, And my mouth offers praises with joyful lips"* (Psalm 63:1-5).

We should pray regularly that we could grow in the discipline — the *sacrifice*, even — of dialing in our focus and attention on God in times of worship.

Stuck

And we should pray that our hearts would be open and free to *respond* with adoring worship to the God who loves us so lavishly and relentlessly! In fact, it's a muscle we should exercise in the privacy of our own prayer corners so we know how to get there quickly on Sunday mornings. That's how we truly *"LOVE THE LORD YOUR GOD WITH ALL YOUR HEART, AND WITH ALL YOUR SOUL, AND WITH ALL YOUR MIND" (Matthew 22:37)*.

Reflect

How are my focus and attention during worship—either personally or corporately? Do I get stuck at *merely* seeing, believing, and proclaiming (praising) and not responding to God in worship? What are some other places I see Christians getting stuck when it comes to worship? How is God leading me to pray about this worship discipline in my own life?

Respond

Lord God, I praise You that You are the One True God, and worthy of every word I could possibly utter in worship to You. Thank You for Your patience with me as I learn to dial in my focus and attention on You. I invite Your Spirit to teach me the way to Your throne. May You find in me a heart that's open and free to responding to You in unbridled worship there. . . . <continue>

DAY TWELVE
Confidence

I've got good news for the discouraged worshiper. Everything you possibly need to be a fully engaged, passionately committed worshiper of God has *already* been given to you. *Everything.* Don't believe otherwise.

God gave you the *Holy Spirit:* **indwelling, guiding, empowering, revealing, interceding, convicting, and transforming.**

(Read that list again considering how *each* word affects your worship life — knowing you'll receive *as much* as you *need* and *allow*.)

And He gave you the *Bible, the Word of God:* **revealing truth, unveiling God, and piercing the soul.**

Because we *can't* do this *worship* thing on our own. We were never supposed to! Just like every other aspect of the Christian life, *"our adequacy is from God"* (2 Corinthians 3:5).

So if you feel inadequate, that's because you *are*. So am I. God never *expected* us to accomplish His purposes and satisfy His will *without* Him. And that includes worship. What He *commands* us to do, He *empowers* us to do. I'm sure you've heard, His *will* always comes with a *way*!

Confidence

And we embrace His *help* by embracing *Him* — embracing a lifestyle of seeking, seeing, believing, loving, and worshiping — *in that order.* That's where we begin.

Seeking → *Seeing* → *Believing* → *Loving* → *Worshiping*

So when it comes to passionately pursuing and intimately engaging the God of the Bible in worship, *stop* trying to do it *on your own* OR giving the responsibility to *somebody else* (like your worship leader).

> Admit your *inadequacies* and accept
> His *provision.*
> Release your *struggles* and welcome
> His *perspective.*
> Forget your *preconceived* ideas and embrace
> His *plan.*
> Stop your *striving* and invite His *power.*
> Give up the *excuses* and pursue His *purpose.*

For "... *we are the true circumcision, who* **worship in the Spirit of God** *and glory in Christ Jesus and put* **no confidence in the flesh**" *(Philippians 3:3).*

The *"My ways are not your ways" (Isaiah 55:8)* truth reaches deep into our *relationship* with God and our *worship of* Him.

I don't know about you, but I'm so glad *His* ways aren't *my* ways. I'm glad that my *limited* view of God isn't all there is. And I'm glad I'm not left to figure out how to get to His throne *confidently* on my own.

Seeking and Savoring

*"For we do not have a high priest who cannot sympathize with our weaknesses, but One who has been tempted in all things as we are, yet without sin. Therefore **let us draw near with confidence to the throne of grace**, so that we may receive mercy and find grace to help in time of need" (Hebrews 4:15-16).*

*"But as for me, **by Your abundant lovingkindness I will enter Your house**, At Your holy temple I will bow in reverence for You" (Psalm 5:7).*

What *grace*. What *love*. What *power*. Everything you possibly need to worship is y*ours*.

Reflect

What would I say my struggles and inadequacies regarding worship are? What truths do I need to claim regarding those struggles? How do I feel God wants to work in my worship life through His Spirit?

Respond

My God, I thank and praise You that Your ways are not like mine. I praise You that You don't leave us on our own to figure out the Christian life or how to worship You as You require. Thank You that You see our weaknesses, yet love us perfectly and continue to draw us close. Help me to move past any limiting views or inadequacies I have

Confidence

that prevent me from drawing near to Your throne of grace with confidence. . . . <continue>

DAY THIRTEEN
Lies

If preventing people from coming to the knowledge of God is the devil's top priority, then sabotaging believers' attempts at *worshiping* Him is probably a close second. Because that defeat not only affects our *own* lives, but also the *Church* — rendering us less effective in the world. But *most* of all, it denies God the *glory* He deserves.

So how does the number one enemy to worship get his job done in the believer's life? He's called the "father of lies" (John 8:44) for a reason! See if any of these lies sound familiar — and don't miss the biblical truths that refute them! (NOTE: Look up these verses in your Bible.)

1. Worship is *for me*. → **TRUTH:** Worship *isn't* about me — or it's *not* worship (of God, at least). (See Psalm 46:10.)

2. My sin doesn't affect my worship. → **TRUTH:** God can't be in the presence of sin — so worship is in *vain*. (See Mark 7:6-7a.)

3. I'm unfit to worship God. → **TRUTH:** Everyone is unfit to worship God apart from His saving grace and forgiveness. (See Hebrews 10:19, 22 and 1 John 1:9.)

Lies

4. God thinks *like me*. → **TRUTH:** God is who He says He is — *infinite, holy,* and *unsearchable.* (See Psalm 50:21 and Romans 11:33, 36.)

5. God doesn't really care if I come. → **TRUTH:** Loving God is demonstrated in many ways, but it's sustained by our *obedience* in worship. (See Luke 4:8.)

6. Worship is a meaningless tradition. → **TRUTH:** Worship is *still* and *will always be* God's purpose for His seeking and saving us. (See Philippians 2:9-11.)

7. Worship is a passive activity I can just observe. → **TRUTH:** Worship in the Bible is defined as something to be engaged in with all our might. (See Romans 14:11.)

8. God won't respond or notice. → **TRUTH:** God *loves* me, *longs to be known* by me, and promises His presence. (See 2 Chronicles 15:2.)

9. Worship makes no difference in my life. → **TRUTH:** Worship brings about a powerful spiritual transformation from the inside out! (See 2 Corinthians 3:18.)

10. Other people are responsible for whether or not I actually worship at church or not. → **TRUTH:** I alone am responsible and can prepare and discipline myself to get past distractions to worship God. (See Psalm 43:3-4a.)

11. My lack of worship doesn't affect the church. → **TRUTH:** True worship *encourages* others in their relationships with God and *reproduces more worship!* (See Psalm 34:2-3.)

Seeking and Savoring

12. It's better that nonbelievers *not* see us worship. → **TRUTH:** The Bible teaches that something supernatural happens when we lift the name of our God for all to see. It exposes His glory and reveals our authenticity. (See Psalm 40:3.)

13. Worship is just for church. → **TRUTH:** There are more examples in the Bible of people worshiping privately. It's the foundation and preparation for corporate worship. (See Psalm 146:1-2.)

14. I can't worship. → **TRUTH:** True worship is the fruit of daily seeking to live in the power of the Holy Spirit — with Him as my guide and the Bible as my road map. (See John 4:23-24.)

Friends, when we fall for these lies, it denies the Creator God of the Universe the worship that *He deserves* — that He *requires*. And it prevents us from fulfilling our *God-given purpose* as worshipers of the Most High God!

It's imperative that we *continually grow to know and love God more* by spending time in His Word and in prayer. *That* is the *fuel* for greater depths of worship *and* the *weapon* to fight Satan's lies.

So be on the alert (1 Peter 5:8)! Know the enemy's schemes so you can quickly deny their power over you! So much is lost — from *God's glory* (first and foremost), to the *transforming power* of Christ, to *unity* in the church — when we *don't* get worship right!

Remember, God's *"abundant lovingkindness"* ushers us into His presence! He *longs* for us to be there!

Lies

"But as for me, by Your abundant lovingkindness I will enter Your house, At Your holy temple I will bow in reverence for You" (Psalm 5:7).

Therefore, "Let us come before His presence with thanksgiving, let us shout joyfully to Him with psalms. For the Lord is a great God . . . " (Psalm 95:2- 3a)!

Reflect

Which lies have I struggled with over the span of my Christian life? Have I struggled with any more recently? Which biblical truths do I feel God leading me to boldly claim over my worship life?

Respond

Lord God, I praise You that You and You only are Truth, and You are far greater than our enemy and his lies. Thank You for giving me everything I need to worship You. Help me to stay on the alert so I don't fall for lies, but allow Your Spirit to usher me to Your throne as You deserve. . . . <continue>

DAY FOURTEEN
Surrender

We're Christians, so we should understand surrender, right? The international sign is both hands up — *You're God, and I'm not.*

Our first act of surrender was when we first accepted Jesus' payment on the cross for our sins and His victorious resurrection — embracing Him as *Savior*. And it continues day after day as we strive to surrender our *will* to His — confessing sin as His Spirit convicts us and choosing His way over ours — making Him *Lord*. So surrender plays a very important part in our daily Christian walk.

And it does in our worship life as well. In fact, the Bible says that only the heart that's surrendered to God can stand before His throne to worship Him.

> *"Who may ascend into the hill of the LORD? And who may stand in His holy place? He who has clean hands and a pure heart, Who has not lifted up his soul to falsehood and has not sworn deceitfully. He shall receive a blessing from the LORD and righteousness from the God of his salvation. This is the generation of those who seek Him, who seek Your face — even Jacob" (Psalm 24:3-6).*

And remember the rich insight Hebrews 10:19, 22 gives us about what kind of heart God requires of His worshipers:

> *"Therefore, brethren, since we have confidence to enter the holy place by the blood of Jesus . . . [Then] Let us draw near with a sincere heart in full assurance of faith, having our hearts sprinkled clean from an evil conscience and our bodies washed with pure water."*

Because worship is never *just* words. It's never just singing, "I surrender all."

Words are merely that—*words*—until poured out from a heart *bowed* before God. And the "bowing" part is what makes it *worship*. **Bowing is the heart's response of submission and surrender to the God it's exalting.** It's lifting God to His rightful place, and then embracing *our* place at His feet.

Worship first involves surrendering our time. It involves surrendering our attention. And then it involves surrendering *all we are* to *all God reveals Himself to be* to us in that place at the foot of His throne.

So in other words:

> It's not enough to declare that God is *holy*. I must surrender all of myself to His *holiness*.

> It's not enough to say that God is my *Lord*. I must surrender all of myself to His *lordship*.

It's not enough to claim that God is my *Rock*. I must surrender all of myself to *stand on* and *trust in* my Rock.

It's not enough to sing the songs of Christ's crucifixion and resurrection. I must *surrender all of myself* to the One who gave His absolute all for me.

And it's in *that* place that gas is thrown on worship's fire—that place of seeing, exalting, embracing, and *surrendering* to *all* of God. It's inviting His Spirit to light the dark places in my soul that don't line up with who He is and saying, "Make me like You!"

As David worshiped—declaring the glory of God and the perfection of His law in Psalm 19—he responded to God with a personal appeal: *"Let the words of my mouth and the meditation of my heart be acceptable in Your sight, O* LORD, *my Rock and my Redeemer" (verse 14).*

May our worship find in us hearts that long to deeply respond to God's Spirit there—surrendering to whatever He reveals of Himself. May we bow *our* all to *His* all.

It's the very sweetest of surrenders. The one that leads to *freedom*. And the *truest* place of worship.

Surrender

Reflect

How do I view surrender as a part of my own personal worship? Do I struggle to surrender my time, attention, or all that I am in worship? Is there an area of my life I struggle to surrender to God on a daily basis? What steps do I need to take to be fully surrendered to God?

Respond

I praise You, my God, for being worthy of my complete surrender. Thank You for shining the Light of Your Spirit on any dark places in my soul so I can see You more clearly. Open my heart and mind to the wonders of Your glory so I might find myself surrendered at Your feet often. May You find in me a heart that longs to surrender and respond to all You are in worship. . . . <continue>

DAY FIFTEEN
Flourish

Do you ever feel overwhelmingly discouraged? Unproductive? Even useless? One day I was paying too much attention to those attacks that say, "Why are you trying so hard? You just don't have much more to offer. Other people are more useful." I could feel my spirit sinking. And then God did that thing He does and quickly led me to this passage:

> *"The righteous man will flourish like the palm tree,*
> *He will grow like a cedar in Lebanon.*
> *Planted in the house of the LORD,*
> *They will flourish in the courts of our God.*
> *They will still yield fruit in old age;*
> *They shall be full of sap and very green,*
> *To declare that the LORD is upright;*
> *He is my rock, and there is no unrighteousness*
> *in Him"* (Psalm 92:12-15).

Peace immediately washed over me as I read, *"Planted in the house of the LORD, they will **flourish** in the courts of our God."* And God whispered, "See, as long as you're planted and nourished in the *house of the Lord*, and if your roots are digging deep in the place of *worship*—in My *"courts"*—then you WILL *"flourish"*! You WILL *thrive!* You don't have to worry about your usefulness. In Me you find all you need. Stop doubting. You will accomplish *all I created you to be and do* when you're planted *in that place* pouring yourself out before Me."

Flourish

Oh, that place—where we can *see* and *bask* in all He's willing to show us of Himself! That place where He makes us like the *"palm tree"* (beautiful and fruitful), the grandest *"cedar"* (fragrant, durable, and long living), as well as *"full of sap and very green."* It's where He fills us with His glory and empowers us to be *all He created us to be!*

AND in the process, glorify Him—as we *"declare"* who He is with our lives! That's the best possible result!

> *"... they will be ... the planting of the* LORD, *that He may be glorified"* (Isaiah 61:3e).

It's so easy to listen to the lies. I've mastered that defeat-bearing task. But the transformational power of being at His feet—focusing on His glory and being reminded of His truth—can lift us to heights that only He can design.

Worship. It's FOR HIM. Period. *But* He pours out all that He is *on us* in the process. His love. His holiness. His goodness. His power. And so much, more. He can't help Himself. And the result? We *flourish*.

Seeking and Savoring

Reflect

Am I in a flourishing place in life? Have I ever experienced the flourishing power of God as a result of worship? How? How do these verses in Psalm 92 encourage my heart today? What's my next step to a flourishing life?

Respond

Lord God, thank You for faithfully leading me to Your Word of truth. I praise You for the power of Your presence when I worship You — that You long to pour out of Your abundance on me when I come. Help me to embrace the truths of Your Word and be found faithful to continually seek after You. Help me to flourish in Your courts as Your worshiper. . . . <continue>

DAY SIXTEEN
Everyday

The Sunday worship disconnect is real. I see and hear about it all the time. I've *been* there! And one of the main causes of it can deceptively sneak past us if we aren't on the alert.

So how about some self-probing questions: *How does the God that I sing about in church compare to the God I allow into my life Monday through Saturday? Is the God I say I worship on Sunday my everyday God?*

For example:

> If I say *You are Lord*, do I let Him have lordship over my life—thoughts, tongue, and actions? (Romans 14:8)
>
> If I say *You are my Healer/Restorer*, do I invite and trust Him to work in my broken places? (1 Peter 5:6-10)
>
> If I say *You are Faithful*, do I still walk in unbelief and anxiety? (Philippians 4:6-7)
>
> If I say *You are my Forgiver*, do I fail to repent of sin or live in guilt? (1 John 1:9)
>
> If I say *You are Holy*, does my life reflect His holiness in every way? (1 Peter 1:15)

Seeking and Savoring

If I say *You are Truth*, do I still listen and walk according to lies? (Psalm 1:1-3)

If I say *You are my Strength*, do I still let my weaknesses overwhelm me? (2 Corinthians 12:9-10)

If I say *I surrender all*, do I still hold tightly to things that I need to give to Him? (Romans 12:1-2)

If I say *I love You, Lord*, do I show that love every day by seeking, obeying, and serving Him? (John 14:21)

Is the God I say I worship on Sunday my *everyday God?*

Acts 17:28a says, *"For in Him we live and move and exist."*

Live and move and exist! I love that all-encompassing thought! I need to *live and move and exist* every day out of *faith* in the all-powerful, living God of the Bible. Not just acknowledge His attributes on Sunday during worship.

So if I feel a disconnect from God in my worship, it might be because there's a discrepancy between the words I *sing* about Him *and* what my heart and mind say I *believe* about Him throughout the week. The good news is that discrepancy can be turned around!

> *"You will seek Me and find Me when you search for Me with all your heart"* (Jeremiah 29:13).

And 1 John 5:14-15 says, *"This is the confidence which we have before Him, that, if we ask anything according to His will, He hears us. And if we know that He hears us in whatever we ask, we know that we have the requests which we have asked from Him."*

Is it God's will for you to know Him and have an intimate *faith-walk* with Him? Yes! Then *ask* for His help! Ask Him to give you the desire to live authentically before Him. Ask for His Holy Spirit to guide you—revealing the Father, shining light on His Word, exposing sin (that breaks your fellowship with Him), and directing your steps. And then *respond in obedience* to whatever He shows you. Living a life where you diligently and continually strive to *know* and *love* your God is the most important step to authentic worship. That's where the *power* lies.

And as you sing words to Him on Sunday morning (that someone else has chosen for you), be in an intentional mental state of praying, *God, help me to see You and grasp these truths about You. Reveal my unbelief and increase my faith. Help me to worship You.*

When your words of worship flow out of a heart that truly *knows* and *believes* they are true, the disconnect will be gone. They will be words to the God you love and seek *every day*. And they will be words that lead you to *true* and *intimate* worship of Him.

Reflect

How does the God that I sing about in church compare to the God I allow into my life Monday through Saturday? Is the God I say I worship on Sunday my everyday God? What comes to mind personally when I read the verse, *"For in Him we live and move and exist."*? How intimate is my faith-walk with Jesus? What steps can I take to make sure I continue to grow in greater intimacy with God?

Respond

My God, thank You that You are mine. Thank You that You desire for me to walk closely with You and have fellowship with You every single day. You long for that. I praise You for Your indescribable love and inexplainable patience You have with me as I strive to grow and understand Your ways. May Your Holy Spirit guide me each day in my seeking and my worship of You. Help me to strive to know and love You more. . . . \<continue\>

DAY SEVENTEEN
Mary

We only run into Mary of Bethany (Martha and Lazarus' sister) a few times in the Bible. And interestingly enough, *every time* she's mentioned, she's in the *exact same place*. And I firmly believe *that place* compelled her worship. But before we talk about Mary's *worship*, we need to look at what *got her there*. Because she's a lot like us — and worship doesn't just *happen*.

We first find Mary in Luke 10:39-42 *sitting at Jesus' feet* while her sister Martha busily prepares dinner. Mary's *"better choice"* (via Jesus) was a place of student to teacher — or even *disciple* to Master — eagerly receiving whatever treasures He had to offer that day. She was *singularly focused* on His *presence*, His *voice*, and His *every word* — all the things that *prepared* her to be His worshiper. And all the things Martha was *"distracted"* from.

Later, Mary is found at Jesus' feet *again* when her brother, Lazarus, died (John 11:1-44), only this time she was pouring out her broken heart at the feet of the only Person she knew could help. The obvious close connection between Mary and Jesus that day — the day *"Jesus wept"* (v. 35) — surely intensified after He raised her beloved brother, and *His friend*, from the dead.

So it's not surprising the Gospel's writers' attention next finds Mary *again* at *Jesus' feet*. (I don't believe for a minute that they were privy to every time she sat there either.) But *this* time, it's different.

> *"Jesus, therefore, six days before the Passover, came to Bethany where Lazarus was, whom Jesus had raised from the dead. So they made Him a supper there, and Martha was serving; but Lazarus was one of those reclining at the table with Him. Mary then took a pound of very costly perfume of pure nard, and anointed the feet of Jesus and wiped His feet with her hair; and the house was filled with the fragrance of the perfume"* (John 12:1-3).

We don't know how much Mary grasped what was waiting for Jesus a mere week away. Regardless, she found herself at His *now-familiar* feet again. Only this time, she wasn't clinging to His words or releasing her sorrow. His feet were now a place of *offering* — of her *lavish surrender, generosity,* and *vulnerability*. It was a place where she was compelled to *sacrifice* from the *best* of her possessions. (As that perfume came at a *cost* — worth close to a year's wages!)

Mary's fragrant offering was one of *extreme* love and devotion. As she culturally *risked* loosening the ties from her hair to wipe His feet, she loosened the ties that held her *very heart*. She wasn't holding back! She didn't care if others were in the room. In her mind, it was just her and Jesus, and she *wasn't* letting this opportunity pass. At those feet, she had tasted of His *wisdom*, His *love*, and His very *resurrection power*. (Can you *even imagine?*) And her compulsion to *respond* to all He meant to her was *overwhelming* in that moment.

Mary

And Jesus loved it. He likened it to preparing Him for burial when Judas scoffed at her *lavishness* (John 12:4-7). Because Jesus knew this was her last chance to be at *these* feet. *"Let her alone" – let her worship Me.*

Want to be a lavish worshiper of the Most High God? Find yourself at His feet—*often*. Say *no* to the distraction of the day, and devote yourself to His *presence*, His *voice*, and His *power-filled word*. Embrace Him as your *Teacher, Master, Savior,* and *Friend*.

And out of *that* place, be drawn to His feet to *respond in worship to all your Savior has revealed to you.*

Out of *that* place, *sacrifice* from the riches He's given you. What's *valuable* to you? Your *time?* Your *attention?* Your *position?* Your very *life? Pour it out.*

Out of *that* place, unleash your highest devotion. *Untie your heart!* Give yourself *radically* to the God who radically gave *Himself* for you on the *cross*.

Then picture Him looking *lovingly* on your loosened heart and the fragrant aroma that's wafting about from your offering. And see Him receiving it with *joy* and saying, *You've chosen the very best.*

Come. I'm waiting. Bring Me your heart. Bring Me your best. This is what I created you for. Worship.

> *"Exalt the LORD our God And worship at His footstool; Holy is He"* (Psalm 99:5).

Reflect

What inspires or encourages me the most about Mary's relationship with Jesus? Do I find myself at His feet often enough? What steps should I take to be a more lavish worshiper of God?

Respond

Lord God, it's unfathomable that You desire for me to sit at Your feet to listen to Your voice and gaze on Your glory. I thank You and praise You for this love I can't comprehend and Your rich mercies that are new every morning. Teach me to be Your lavish worshiper. Strengthen me to say "no" to distractions so I might devote myself to Your presence.... <continue>

DAY EIGHTEEN
Vision

In high school, I had a friend named Al who had tunnel vision. He had no peripheral vision, so his eyes quickly darted back and forth all the time as he tried to catch the whole picture in front of him. He could only see where he was directly looking. His vision was constricted and concentrated on *one thing at a time*.

I believe God *wants* us to have tunnel vision for *Him* in our times of worship.

He wants us to stop the eyes of our hearts and minds from darting back and forth, so we can temporarily forget everything around us and *see only Him*. Nurturing that ability to focus completely and exclusively on God is important to achieving the worship intimacy He so desires from us.

One of my favorite Greek words for *worship* is *proskuneo*, and it literally means "to bow and kiss." Imagine how impossible it would be to get ourselves to a place of submissively bowing and kissing the feet of Jesus if we couldn't get our focus off of everything else going on around us! You can't kiss someone you're not looking at! True worship requires a focus that's *all encompassing* — the attention and response of *all I am*.

Seeking and Savoring

I believe that tunnel vision for God only happens as a by-product of *stillness*.

Stillness these days is increasingly difficult to come by, it seems. But we must view it as nonnegotiable for gaining knowledge and intimacy with God. It's crucial for calming the heart and mind. And it's crucial for truly seeing and hearing.

We gain nothing with the drive-by glance mentality when it comes to our relationship to God. Our heavenly Father is always calling us to Himself, saying, *Come to me. Be still and commune with My Spirit. Let Me pour out My love and grace over you. Come often. Stay long. Be still. I have so much for you here.*

> *"Be still, and know that I am God" (Psalm 46:10a, ESV).*

And the second half of that verse shows the incredible results of being still. *"Be still, and know that I am God.* **I will be exalted among the nations, I will be exalted in the earth!"** *(Psalm 46:10, ESV).* Worship!

Worship is the result of achieving glorious tunnel vision for your God—which is born out of stillness. It's born out of seeking, seeing, and responding to Him *alone*. Worship out of *that* place is the worship that God so longs for from us.

> *"When You said, 'Seek My face,' my heart said to You, 'Your face, O LORD, I shall seek' " (Psalm 27:8).*

Vision

Reflect

What do I see as my greatest enemy to having tunnel vision for God in worship? What makes the eyes of my heart and mind dart around instead of focusing on Him? Do I struggle with the discipline of being still before God? How do I feel God leading me to work on this area of my walk with Him and worship life?

Respond

Thank You for longing to commune with me in a place of stillness and intimacy. I praise You for Your love and grace that flow in abundance toward me. Help me to learn how to have tunnel vision for You in my worship. Help me to learn how to stop my eyes and mind from darting around to see and focus on other, lesser things. But help me to learn to quiet my soul and calm my mind for truly seeing and hearing You. . . . <continue>

*This devotion includes excerpts from my book, *Worship and the Word*.

DAY NINETEEN
Passivity

I don't think most people go to church on Sunday saying to themselves, *I'm just going to passively worship God today.* I think it mostly just happens by default. Am I wrong?

I'm not saying passive worship is everyone's experience. But I've heard the comments, and I remember that default worship setting I had for many years of my own Christian walk. I just didn't know differently!

Now, the problem of not engaging in worship isn't a new one at all.

> *"And He said to them, 'Rightly did Isaiah prophesy of you hypocrites, as it is written: This people honors Me with their lips, but their heart is far away from Me. But in vain do they worship Me" (Mark 7:6-7a).*

But I believe our current culture has shoved it off the cliff. We struggle to engage with *others* in the same room! Plus we're programmed to want *easy*. If we can't check our device for a quick answer, we don't bother. So through *observation* and *repetition*, we've grown to *believe* Christian worship is merely a *passive* activity. We stand, we sing, so we've done our part. (And I don't often hear pastors teaching otherwise.)

Passivity

But the norm of *unengaged* and *unresponsive* worship is the *opposite* of what the Bible teaches. That's indisputable when we look up the original meanings of the words for worship used in the Bible. Here are a few.

Hebrew:

> **HALAL** – expresses an unbridled, exuberant worship: *"My soul **will make its boast** in the Lord" (Psalm 34:2).*
>
> **SHACHAH** – bowing down before: *"Come, let us **worship** and bow down" (Psalm 95:6).*
>
> **YADAH** – from two words that mean "to extend the hand" and "to God," in *adoration* or *surrender*: *"My heart trusts in Him, and I am helped; Therefore my heart exults, And with my song I **shall thank** Him" (Psalm 28:7b).*

Greek:

> **PROSKUNEO** – "to bow and kiss" in humble adoration: *"But an hour is coming, and now is, when the true **worshipers** shall **worship** the Father in spirit and truth; for such people the Father seeks to be His **worshipers**. God is spirit; and those who **worship** Him must **worship** in spirit and truth" (John 4:23-24).*

I just don't see anything passive there. Because if it's *passive*, it's not *worship*. True worship goes far beyond singing (or even enjoying) the songs to the *complete surrender and engagement of our hearts, minds, and souls* to

Seeking and Savoring

the God *those words should be lifted to*. It's offering *all* of myself to *all* of God.

So now what?

The number one way out of the passive rut is to *run from* the habitual fallacy of passive worship to *chase after the God who deserves more*. **We need to stop being satisfied with doing this the easy way (which isn't doing it at all), and get caught up in the absolute *otherness* of the God we stand before—that we're supposed to *bow* before.**

We need to carve new, deep, neural pathways in our brains with a *daily striving* to know, understand, and be awestruck by the *otherness* of God. Pathways that compel us *toward* Him. Pathways that move the depths of our souls to declare in any given moment,

> "I will extol You, my God, O King, And I will bless Your name forever and ever. Every day I will bless You, And I will praise Your name forever and ever. Great is the LORD, and highly to be praised, And His greatness is unsearchable" (Psalm 145:1-3).

That God—our mighty, unfathomable, unsearchable, ever-faithful, all-loving *(and so much more)* God—is who we need to place before us when we come to worship. *That* God is who we need to *responsively bow* our *hearts and minds* (and yes, sometimes our *knees*) before in worship. And *that* God is who requires we do so! Don't settle for giving Him less!

Passivity

Let's *run from* the fallacy of passive worship and *chase after* the God who deserves far more. Let's chase after *God!*

Reflect

How do these Hebrew and Greek definitions affect how I think about worship? Do I struggle to engage fully with God during times of worship? How can I build new habits that compel me to engage more fully? What goals should I set in this area?

Respond

Lord God, I praise You for being our mighty, unfathomable, unsearchable, ever-faithful, all-loving God. Thank You for being worthy of everything I could conceivably offer You in worship. May Your Spirit nudge me when I'm merely mouthing words to You and not surrendering my heart and mind in worship. Help me to be committed to responding with all I am to all You are. . . . <continue>

DAY TWENTY
Drink

One morning I was reading my Bible when Psalm 36 leapt out to offer me a renewing perspective. It's easy to get lost in the beautiful pictures David paints of his intimacy with his Lord. And Psalm 36 is one of those.

First, you need to know this psalm begins as quite the downer about the *"sinfulness of the wicked" (v. 1)* — something we're not oblivious to these days. But David quickly adjusted his own perspective in vv. 5-6 with *"Your love, Lord, reaches to the heavens, your faithfulness to the skies. Your righteousness is like the highest mountains, your justice like the great deep" (NIV)*. Ahh . . . (anyone else hearing Third Day in your head all of a sudden?)

Then as He continues, my smile gets even wider:

> *"They drink their fill of the abundance*
> *of Your house;*
> *And You give them to drink of the river*
> *of Your delights.*
> *For with You is the fountain of life;*
> *In Your light we see light" (vv. 8-9).*

I stopped right there, because I suddenly felt the need to grasp what all was in *"the abundance of [His] house"* that I was invited to drink of. And I wanted to fathom what

Drink

could possibly wash over me from *"the river of [His] delights."* I began a list—God's majesty, beauty, grace, mercy, faithfulness, truth, love, hope, peace, compassion, joy, strength—but quickly realized that it was *"too amazing for me. It is beyond my reach, and I cannot fathom it"* ... (borrowing from David's Psalm 139, v. 6, ISV).

Yet, He beckons us to not only *"drink"*—but to *"drink [our] fill of the abundance."* He delights in pouring Himself out for us—as much as we can possibly handle. So much so, David calls it the *"fountain of life"* and the place where we find the much-needed *"light"* in *"[His] light."*

I'm more than just a little overwhelmed by these thoughts. Overwhelmed by the *inconceivable "abundance"* that He offers me, and overwhelmed that He *so graciously chooses* to offer it to me. To *me*.

IF I but *"drink."* How often have I passed up on this heavenly fountain? <*sigh*>

Then I saw in the margin of my Bible next to this passage, I had written "Psalm 43:3-4," so I quickly flipped there:

> *"O send out Your light and Your truth,*
> *let them lead me;*
> *Let them bring me to Your holy hill*
> *And to Your dwelling places.*
> *Then I will go to the altar of God,*
> *To God my exceeding joy;*
> *And upon the lyre I shall praise You,*
> *O God, my God."*

Ahh! As we relish in the *"light"* that our God pours out for us (as we first read in Psalm 36), it *"leads"* us to *"[His] holy hill"* to worship at His *"altar"*! His *"river of delights"* blesses us indeed—*lavishly*. But *more importantly*, it compels us to the point of *actually ushering us to the place of worship!*

Again—IF we but *"drink."*

Struggle to worship—whether you're at church or at home? Then you may be *thirsty*. Get in God's love letter to you and *"drink [your] fill."* Sit quietly and meditate on all He reveals to you there. Bask in His presence. Ask His Spirit to lead you to the *"abundance of [His] house"* and the *"river of [His] delights"* so you can *"drink"*—and then drink *some more*. Commit to *never stop drinking!*

For in that place of the unspeakable *"abundance"* and *"delights"* of God and His grace is where you'll find *that which will make you* an absolute insatiable worshiper of the Most High God.

Drink!

Reflect

How would I describe the *"river of [God's] delights"*? Or *"the abundance of [His] house"*? How do these passages inspire my worship life? Can I commit to *never stop drinking* from the river of His delights?

Drink

What steps is God leading me to take that are inspired by these verses?

Respond

My God, thank You for the abundance of Your house that You offer me every single day. I praise You for Your generous grace that makes it possible for me to draw near to You to drink. Help me to embrace Your light and truth so they might lead me to a place of intimate worship. And help me to drink my fill of the river of Your delights. May my inability to grasp these truths not prevent me from coming often to Your Word and Your throne. Increase my picture and reverence for You. . . . <continue>

DAY TWENTY-ONE
Grace

I was in a frustrated funk. I'd been working hard on something for some time, but it wasn't going as I'd hoped. And as I *unwisely* allowed my focus to veer *off* the road God had paved with confidence, I began questioning all the important whys, whats, and hows attached to what I was doing. I was tired, confused, demoralized, and frankly, lonely in my labor.

Then a short phrase in a familiar verse grabbed not only my attention *but* also my weary heart.

> "But by the grace of God I am what I am, and His grace toward me did not prove vain; but **I labored even more than all of them, yet not I, but the grace of God with me**" (1 Corinthians 15:10).

There's no way I could recall the number of times I'd read that verse before. But on a day when I was *mistakenly feeling alone* in my labor (*I knew better!*), the timely reminder that *God's grace was laboring with me* took my breath away. While it wasn't an unfamiliar truth at all, the overwhelming thought of the *unmerited favor of God laboring in, through, and beside me* made me instantly dig deeper for more "*grace*" gold.

I quickly journaled verse after verse of the sometimes forgotten treasure that is *God's grace*. And wouldn't you know it, I was lovingly pointed toward *worship*. (Shocked?)

I invite you to soak in a few of the many verses I found that day to be reminded of — or *maybe* discover for the first time — the *staggering place of grace* in your worship. The incomprehensible, unmerited, undeserved favor of God is truly *grace upon grace upon grace*.

God's grace . . .

1) Makes me what I am.

> *"But **by the grace of God I am what I am**, . . ."* (1 Corinthians 15:10a).

2) Is sufficient for me.

> *"And God is able to **make all grace abound to you**, so that always **having all sufficiency in everything**, you may have an abundance for every good deed;"* (2 Corinthians 9:8).

3) Makes it possible for me to glorify Him.

> *" . . . so that the name of our Lord Jesus will be glorified in you, and you in Him, **according to the grace of our God** and the Lord Jesus Christ"* (2 Thessalonians 1:12).

Seeking and Savoring

4) Is the very name of His throne!

> *"For we do not have a high priest who cannot sympathize with our weaknesses, but One who has been tempted in all things as we are, yet without sin. Therefore let us **draw near with confidence to the throne of grace**, so that we may receive mercy and find grace to help in time of need" (Hebrews 4:15-16).*

Friend, *worship* is the *grace*-infused, surrendered response of *all I am* to all God is and does — and *God made me all I am*! (Read that again.)

I don't know about you, but I need to meditate on these *grace*-truths a *lot* more often. God's word teaches us that *grace* is something that can be multiplied (2 Peter 1:2) and even be transferrable (2 Corinthians 4:15). (*How are we doing at that?*) It's also something we can grow in <*yes!*> (2 Peter 3:17-18) or fall short in <*ouch!*> (Hebrews 12:15).

So when I come to the throne as a *grace*-saved (Ephesians 2:8-9), *grace*-justified (Titus 3:7), *grace*-made, *grace*-called (2 Timothy 1:9), *grace*-empowered (1 Peter 5:10) believer, I'm only pouring back out to my *grace*-giving God all He has lavished on me through His *astonishing unmerited favor* to begin with! *He alone* makes me *acceptable* to come before Him and makes it *possible* for me to glorify Him *at* His *throne of grace!* How overwhelmingly humbling!

> *"For of His fullness we have all received, and grace upon grace" (John 1:16).*

Grace

Reflect

How do I need to grow in my understanding of God's grace as it applies to my life and/or worship? Which one of these verses on God's grace stands out to me the most today? Which grace promise do I need to claim today?

Respond

Lord God, I thank and praise You for your overwhelming, life-enveloping, soul-infusing grace. Help me count on Your grace, grow in Your grace, and transfer Your grace to others. I humbly bow all You've given and made me to be before Your very throne of grace and give You all the glory in Jesus' name. . . . <continue>

DAY TWENTY-TWO
Remember

Memory is a powerful motivator. What we focus on most obviously fills the most active parts of our minds. **But the things we *cherish* the deepest will *compel* us the greatest.**

God tells us over and over in His Word to remember. *Remember.* Even things that we should never conceivably forget, still we're told again, *remember.* Why? Because our all-knowing, all-wise God knows how easily we forget—how easily we're distracted or deceived. And He knows far better than we do how important it is.

In Joshua 4:7, God had the Israelites take twelve stones from the middle of the Jordan so they would *remember* what He did for them there. He didn't want them to *ever* forget. The stones were reminders they could literally see and touch that screamed *our God is faithful!*

Similarly, Jesus instructed us to take communion just so we would continue to *remember* what He did for us on the cross (1 Corinthians 11:23-25). This foundational sacrament is a powerful reminder that engages our entire being—that we can see, touch, and even taste.

Personally, I love having reminders I can see and touch. I treasure the pictures in the photo albums in my house

Remember

that tell the story of our family and friends and bring back a flood of emotions with them.

And I think it's more important to have reminders of our God story. That's one reason I journal nearly daily, and will even bookmark key days when God showed me something powerful from His Word or I felt Him intervene in a very real way. Because like the Israelites, I'm sure there are things He doesn't want me to ever forget. And because *worship* always involves *remembering* and *responding*. Proclaiming You are who You say You are, and surrendering at His feet.

So it's important when the tough times come that our most powerful memory reminds us, But You are . . . , or But You say. . . .

It's important when the blessings come that we're quick to say, You have been faithful to . . . , and You are good.

And it's important as we observe His spectacular creation around us that our first response proclaims, You, my God are mighty. . . . There is no one like You.

This only happens if my thoughts of God are fresh, real, and strong. There's no comparison between the power and intimacy in my times of worship when my God-memory is strong—and when it's *just not*. In the former, I can quickly get to the foot of the throne and pour out all that my God deserves in His presence. And in the latter, the distractions are strong, the memories a struggle, and the intimacy just not there. That's not true worship.

We need to do *whatever it takes* to KNOW and REMEMBER the One True God that we're called to worship. We should ask His Spirit to help us remember (John 14:26), but also take steps to record His goodness, faithfulness, and power — in the past and present and in the large or small. We need to remember *who our God is* and *who He has always has been.*

Let's follow Asaph's example in Psalm 77:11-13 (NIV) when he said, *"I will remember the deeds of the Lord; yes, I will remember your miracles of long ago. I will consider all your works and meditate on all your mighty deeds. Your ways, God, are holy. What god is as great as our God?"*

Be intentional about remembering! He deserves nothing less.

Reflect

What steps do I already take to intentionally remember what God has done — past and present? How is God leading me to respond to the challenging verses about remembering? How should I let that influence my walk with God and worship?

Respond

Thank You, God, for Your Word's reminder to remember everything You are to me. I praise You for Your

Remember

faithfulness, goodness, and grace over the course of my life. Help me to often remember all You have done — from the cross to today — and respond with whole-hearted worship. . . . <continue>

DAY TWENTY-THREE
Breath

I'm frequently struck by how *under*whelmed I can seem by incredible truths about God. Things that should literally take my breath away, I'm guilty of merely glancing at and then looking away. *As if anything about God could ever become ordinary or unworthy of my full attention.* So I love it when He breaks through my distraction of the moment to woo me to His heart and open my mind to His absolute, greater wonders.

Example—we all do it. *Breathe.* But how often do we stop to think about where that breath comes from *and* what we do with it *given* where it comes from?

We are told from the beginning that *"the* Lord *God formed man of dust from the ground, and* **breathed into his nostrils the breath of life;** *and man became a living being"* (Genesis 2:7).

Job declared, *"the* **breath of God** *is in my nostrils"* (Job 27:3).

And Acts 17:25b says, *"He Himself gives to all people life and* **breath** *and all things."*

We read and know this *intellectually*. But how often do we allow ourselves to be captured by the power and

Breath

wonder of that truth? That it's *God's very breath* filling our lungs! And we literally use His breath *in* us to pour our praise and worship *out* in response to Him. Think about that for a minute. And consider how every day is full of *choices* of how to use that God-given breath — to *worship* Him with our lives and voices, or *not*. It's staggering.

Psalm 150:6 says, *"Let everything that has **breath** praise the* L*ord*. *Praise the* L*ord!"*

And Psalm 104:33 (NLT), *"I will sing to the* L*ord as long as I live. I will praise my God **to my last breath**!"*

And of course, we could take it a step further, and consider what Psalm 135:15, 17-18 has to add to the conversation: *"The idols of the nations are but silver and gold, the work of man's hands. . . . They have ears, but they do not hear,* ***Nor is there any breath*** *at all in their mouths. Those who make them **will be like them**, yes, everyone who **trusts in them**."* Yikes! Not only do our misplaced affections not have breath, but those who trust in them will become like them — with no breath!

Each of us should invite God to overwhelm us with *this* simple, yet powerful, truth — *His breath in me*. And allow God to take the very breath He *gave* us *away* in worship!

Reflect

When have I had a moment when God captured my heart with a simple, but powerful, truth about Himself? How do I feel knowing God's very breath is in me? What can I do to spend more time focused on the incredible wonders of God?

Respond

Oh God, I praise You that You are the only true God who is alive! And I praise You for the incredible truth that Your very breath is inside me. Thank You for giving me breath and life and every good thing. Overwhelm me with the simple, powerful truths that are around me every day. May I be worthy of Your breath, and use it to worship You as long as I live. . . . <continue>

DAY TWENTY-FOUR
Silence

Is *silence* a struggle for you?

Apparently you're not alone. If you do a quick google search on "the need for silence," there are a bazillion articles on the topic. And some even say we need silence to *survive*!

What about *silence* and the *survival* of our relationship with *God*? I believe regular *silence* is a vital, missing link in a lot of people's walk with God *and* their worship *of* Him. I know it's one of mine. Just being honest.

David's opening verse in Psalm 65 got the *silence* topic churning in my head recently.

> *"There will be **silence before You**, and praise in Zion, O God,*
>   *And to You the vow will be performed. . . .*
>
> *How blessed is the one whom You choose and bring near to You*
>   *To dwell in Your courts.*
>   *We will be satisfied with the goodness of Your house,*
>   *Your holy temple"* (Psalm 65:1, 4).

Seeking and Savoring

I love the picture David paints of *silence before God* either *preceding* or *being part of* praising Him. Because it's in silence that God is *free* to speak into our quieted hearts and stilled minds. *Silence* gives Him the much-needed *space* to remind us who He is and draw us closer and into an intimate time of worship.

Shhhh, I AM.

What does silence accomplish?

1) Silence before God encourages REST.

I don't mean sleep (fight it if you're tempted!), but *resting in who God is.* Silence allows the heart, mind, and soul to slow down enough to soak in the presence of God. *I am here. So is God. And I have no other agenda other than being with Him* – leaning into His presence.

> "My soul waits in silence for God only; From Him is my salvation" (Psalm 62:1).

2) Silence before God induces REVERENCE.

In my silence I acknowledge that He is God and I am not. I *bow my heart* before all He is – known and unknown – and *surrender my all.* Silence prepares the soil of my heart to be awed by God.

> ". . . let us offer to God acceptable worship, with reverence and awe," (Hebrews 12:28b).

Silence

3) Silence before God rouses ANTICIPATION.

He loves it when we *long* for Him and *wait* on Him. God desperately wants to draw us into an intimate relationship with Himself. And that can't happen apart from silence. It's where hope is fueled. And it's where He *"bring(s) [us] near"* to *"satisfy [us] with the goodness of [His] house" (Psalm 65:4).*

> *"My soul, wait in silence for God only, For my hope is from Him" (Psalm 62:5).*

4) Silence before God inspires WORSHIP.

All of these lead us to a place of offering back to God in worship all He's poured out for us. *I humbly give You all I am in response to all You are.* Because sometimes earthly words are just sorely inadequate for responding to our unsearchable God, and *humbly lavish silence expresses it best.*

> *"But the* LORD *is in His holy temple. Let all the earth be silent before Him" (Habakkuk 2:20).*

I know it's a battle. But I want that time of silence before God to become like daily air that I can't survive without—because it so fills my soul, and most of all, because God deserves it.

What's the surest way to give God glory? Bowed-down, humbled-before-Him, opened-to-Him, lavish *silence* expresses it best.

Seeking and Savoring

Reflect

Do I struggle with silence? Which of these points or verses encourages my worship of God the most? What steps should I take to grow in my time of silence before God?

Respond

Lord God, I love how You long to speak into our stilled hearts and minds. I praise You for the power of Your presence in the quiet spaces. May I give You the much-needed space You deserve to remind me who You are and to draw me closer still. Teach me to respond to Your powerful presence with worship. . . . <continue>

DAY TWENTY-FIVE
Battles

None of us are immune from the spiritual battles of life. And not surprisingly, the enemy's fingerprints are usually all over them. So these times threaten to weigh us down with thoughts and emotions that aren't remotely defined by *"love, joy, peace, patience, . . ." (Galatians 5:22)* — if we're not prepared.

I remember *finally* relenting from trying to figure out a certain situation (ridiculous attempt) and prayed, "What do You want me to do?" I didn't pray it as calmly as you probably just read it. There was a hint of desperation in my voice. I had obviously allowed myself to go further down a dark side road than I should have.

And my always patient, loving God responded to my soul with, *Look — at — Me. In Me you will always find truth, peace, and strength. Stop looking all around and focus right here — on Me. I am all you need. I will guide your next step. Stay here.*

What a soothing balm those words were to my soul. As many times as I've proclaimed those foundational truths myself, I obviously needed to hear them again. **I was reminded in that moment of the power of gazing on my Lord and bowing to Him** *instead* **of my circumstances.**

Seeking and Savoring

The Bible is full of examples when people found the barrier-breaking power of worship when they came face-to-face with God—the God who sees, the God who knows, the God who overcomes, God our Rock—in their difficult places of life.

David wrote Psalm 63 when he was in the wilderness of Judah. Obviously, the place David is in at this point in his life isn't all that great. God was protecting him, but He hadn't changed his situation yet. David knows his need to seek God, and seeks Him *"earnestly" (v. 1)*. He does this by entering the *"sanctuary" (v. 2)*, or place of worship, *"to see [His] power and [His] glory" (v. 2)*.

Why? Because he already knows by experience that God's *"lovingkindness is better than life" (v. 3)*, and he knows his need to verbalize it once more. After all, his *"life"* was on the line *(v. 9)*!

So this was David's expression of faith and the beginning of worship to the God that he intimately knew. As David continues to lift up who God is, he finds *"satisfaction" (v. 5)* for his soul. He then continues to *"remember" (v. 6)* God's faithfulness and strength in the past, leading to an increase in his faith and reliance on God for his current, difficult situation.

We begin to feel defeat *"in the dry and weary land" (v. 1)*, when we fail to recognize that we *"thirst"* and *"yearn" (v. 1)* for God. We don't strive to *"see" (v. 2)* Him there and, therefore, fail to drink to quench our thirst. We don't *"remember" (v. 6)* who He is and, therefore, fail to worship Him. The end result is we fail to find the *"satisfaction" (v. 5)*, increased faith, strength, and even *"joy" (v. 7)* that God makes available to us.

David wasn't in denial about his situation. He was living in the midst of the reality of *who God was for him* in that situation. That reality was only found because David chose to worship in the good times *preparing* himself for the bad.

May the battles of life find in us hearts that comprehend the power of God's presence and glory in worship and, therefore, *choose* to bow before Him once again.

Reflect

What's an example of when my regular worship prepared me for one of the battles of life? When has God pulled me out of one of life's pits as a result of turning to worship? How is my view of being prepared to worship in difficult times encouraged or challenged?

Seeking and Savoring

Respond

My God, I thank You and praise You for your patience, love, and gentleness towards me when I'm in a difficult place. Thank You for always drawing me back to Your presence and to a place of increased peace, strength, and even joy. Remind me of my need to keep seeking You. Remind me of my need to savor every glance You give me of who You are – of Your glory. . . . <continue>

DAY TWENTY-SIX
Paul

I love the study of biblical worshipers, because what we learn from them could have *huge* implications on our lives—*if* we let it. And the story of Paul and Silas in Acts 16:16-34 is no exception.

To quickly set up the story, Paul and Silas were just doing what they do—casting out an evil spirit from a fortune-teller on their way to pray. (Just another day.) But that helpful move more than upset the men who were profiting from this poor woman's affliction. So they seized the two God-proclaiming men, had them severely beaten, and then thrown in a guarded prison cell with their feet in stocks. (Realize, Paul was stoned and left for dead just two chapters earlier!) Their pain is severe—physically and emotionally.

So what do they do?

> "But about midnight Paul and Silas were praying and singing hymns of praise to God, and the prisoners were listening to them" (Acts 16:25).

Before we continue, I think we need **a quick flashback:** Paul, if you remember, was raised (as Saul) a devout, well-educated Jew. Beyond that, he was a hater, persecutor, and murderer of Christians—even watching and

Seeking and Savoring

applauding Stephen's stoning. And *that* history, leading up to his dramatic, Damascus-road run-in with God, is why he called himself *"the foremost of sinners"* (*1 Timothy 1:15-16*).

Friends, **Paul never, ever got over the unfathomable mercy and grace of the God that saved him.** (Read his letters—he can't stop talking about God's *grace!*) And beyond propelling his ministry, *it fueled his worship*. It compelled him to his knees even in the very worst of times.

He *never* forgot where he came from. And more importantly, he never forgot *who God was for him* in *that* place or any *new* place life might (*literally*) throw him.

So back at the prison—this was a truly amazing moment. Their worship was not a response that poured out from any of their expected reactions or emotions. (Anxiety? Fear? Anger? How about hopelessness, discontentment, self-centeredness, powerlessness, faithlessness, and a whole slew of other negative responses that we could come up with?) This was the response of men who *knew, loved, and still trusted their grace-filled God* in spite of their circumstances.

This was the response of men who knew that their *only* source of strength in their weakness, and their *only* source of grace in their agony, was the God whom they worshiped with their whole hearts.

We can only imagine the intense prayers that poured from their lips that night. But we know that their God was present and attentive, and that He ministered to their battered *bodies, minds, and souls*. And out of that place of much-needed grace came their heart-felt songs of praise to Him.

Of course, God responded to their grace-fueled worship other ways that night. CliffsNotes version: He sent an earthquake that unfastened everyone's chains, and the jailer and his family were all saved that night! (Reminds me of David's Psalm 40:3, *"He put a new song in my mouth, a song of praise to our God; Many will see and fear And will trust in the LORD."* Wonder if they were thinking of that verse as they sang?)

What can *we* learn from the grace-fueled worship of Paul?

We should pray that, like Paul, we *never, ever get over the unfathomable mercy and grace of the God that saved us*, and allow that to *overwhelm* our souls and *fuel* our *worship*. *Whenever. Wherever.*

Regardless of what our chains look like, *God is still God*. He never changes. His mercies are new every morning, and His grace is unending. And there is *transformation power* when we choose to *remember who God is* and *worship Him*.

For He alone is worthy of our praise!

> *"I will sing of the mercies of the LORD for ever: with my mouth will I make known Your faithfulness to all generations"* (Psalm 89:1, NKJV).

Seeking and Savoring

Reflect

What part of this story about Paul and Silas stirs in my soul the most? Do I have "chains" that prevent me from worshiping God? What are they? How do I sense God calling me to respond to the powerful message from Paul and Silas' jail cell worship?

Respond

Lord God, I thank and praise You for the unfathomable mercy and grace that saved me and still surrounds me each and every day. Help me to remember who You are at all times. And may I allow that knowledge to overwhelm my soul and draw me to Your feet in worship. . . .
<continue>

---

*This devotion includes excerpts from my book, *Worship and the Word*.

DAY TWENTY-SEVEN
Talk

What we tell ourselves is important. We all know the results of negative self-talk and how important it is to replace those thoughts with positive, encouraging words.

That goes for our spiritual and worship life as well. David had it figured out when he said to himself,

> *"Bless the LORD, O my soul, And all that is within me, bless His holy name.*
>
> *Bless the LORD, O my soul, And forget none of His benefits"* (Psalm 103:1-2).

He then went on to list the *mercies* God had poured out in his own life as well as in the lives of others.

I don't think this was just an intellectual exercise on David's part. I think it was the prompting of the Holy Spirit reminding him of his *need* – his need to literally *command* himself to *"Bless the Lord!"*

Maybe he was struggling to believe truth in a hard place. Maybe he was battling negative thoughts. But he stopped dead in his tracks and said, *"Listen soul, you need to bless the Lord! Don't forget who He is or what He's done!"* (my paraphrase).

Seeking and Savoring

David wasn't the only one. Here's some more self-talk from the psalmists:

> *"Why are you in despair, O my soul? And why have you become disturbed within me?* **Hope in God**, *for I shall again praise Him for the help of His presence"* (Psalm 42:5).

> **"Bless the LORD, O my soul!** *O LORD my God, You are very great; You are clothed with splendor and majesty"* (Psalm 104:1).

> **"Praise the LORD! Praise the LORD, O my soul!** *I will praise the LORD while I live; I will sing praises to my God while I have my being. Do not trust in princes, In mortal man, in whom there is no salvation"* (Psalm 146:1-3).

(Good self-reminder at the end of who *not* to trust in!)

Or sometimes we just need to start with **"Wake up, my soul!"** *(Psalm 57:8, CSB).*

We *all* have those times when worship is clearly a struggle. Life has done its thing to us, and we just don't seem to have the focus or energy we need to think clearly, much less *worship*. That's when we need to stop, and respond to the Spirit of God's inevitable prompting to have the right kind of talk with ourselves:

Remember *who your God is* **and worship** *Him! He's who you need to see right now. He is your truth, light, hope, and peace in this place. Remember and pour yourself out to Him now. Invite His Spirit to replace your thoughts with all that*

Talk

He is. Confess your sin. Release your weaknesses and burdens. Give Him all that you carry and all that you are. Pour it out at His feet and soak in His presence. He is all you need. He alone is worthy of all you have to offer Him.

There are many things that can derail us on this journey of being a worshiper of our great God. Thankfully, they can all be diverted by Spirit-led self-talk. *Remember* who He is. *Remember* what He's done. *Bless* the Lord!

Reflect

How do I handle the times I need a "Wake up, soul!" moment? How do these verses encourage me in the times I can't seem to focus on worshiping God? What step is God leading me to take in response?

Respond

My God, I praise You that You are worthy of all the praise I could ever offer You. I thank and praise You for Your Holy Spirit that indwells me, guides me, and encourages me. Make me sensitive to His voice that prompts me when I need a wake-up call to seek You and worship You. Teach me to stop and focus on You when I so desperately need it — because You alone are worthy. . . . <continue>

DAY TWENTY-EIGHT
Give

"Give Me what you have."

That's what Jesus said to the disciples who had just described their quite insignificant loaves and fish to Him (Matthew 14:13-21). Just *give Me what you have.* We all know that popular Bible story and the incredible ending. But what's our response when God says to *us*, "Give Me what you have — as inadequate as you think it is"? Do we focus on what we obviously don't have (oh, the enemy's voice is strong!), or do we *remember the truth about what **He** can do*? (Even the disciples quickly forgot.)

I've fought that lie of not having or being enough. I know what is required (or *think* I do), and trust me, I don't always have it. Not by a long shot. But my oh-so-patient heavenly Father keeps saying, "Just give it to Me anyway. Trust Me to work. Trust Me to accomplish what concerns you (Psalm 138:8) with what you have." And the stories I could tell — of God receiving my meager offering (which *He gave* to me to begin with, remember) and then pouring out His grace and power to make it much more usable — make my eyes well up with tears. And the end result? More glory to Himself!

If worship is the surrendered response of everything I am to everything God is, then that offering of *everything*

I am obviously includes a *lot* of seemingly insignificant gifts. Of the use of our spiritual gifts in 1Peter 4:11, it says, *"by the strength that God supplies, so that in all things God may be glorified through Jesus Christ."* That's the result we should all desire: God's strength → God's glory.

So God is glorified in that place of surrendered *obedience* and absolute *trust* at His feet. Trust in the *love* He receives our seemingly insignificant gift with. Trust in the value *He* places on our gift. And trust in *His* ability and desire to use the gift—*however* that looks. It needs to be all about *Him*. That's what makes it worship.

And what indescribable joy when God receives the meager offering and makes it not only sufficient but *more than enough* for His purposes—like the loaves and fish. Go ahead and try to imagine the impact not only on your life but also on that of others! It's part of living a life of worship. *"Just give Me what you have."* In each of life's moments—*and* at the foot of His throne. He requires and deserves it all.

Reflect

What are my stories of struggle or victory when responding to God's invitation to "just give Me what you have"? How should I view my meager offerings in light of what God calls me to give—especially remembering He gave it to me to begin with?

Seeking and Savoring

Respond

My God, I thank You for Your unconditional love and faithfulness towards me. I thank You for working in and through my meager gifts to bring glory to Yourself. Show me where I'm believing lies about myself or about what You long to accomplish in and through me. Help me to open my hands in faith to offer You everything I have. Help me to worship You with everything I am. . . .
<continue>

DAY TWENTY-NINE
Apathy

My heart sank when I heard these words come out of a friend's mouth. "That's okay, worship isn't how I connect with God anyway."

It was said casually in response to someone expressing regret our friend had missed out on the worship at a small gathering. And there didn't seem to be much thought as to what that sentiment really meant—as if they were okay missing out on the pizza.

Would it surprise you if I revealed it was a comment by someone in ministry?

Just because someone loves and serves God doesn't mean they're inoculated against worship *ignorance* or *apathy*. I wish it did, because I know the benefits to their personal and ministry life would be incalculable.

The misunderstanding and undereducation regarding what the Bible teaches us about worship continues to baffle and sadden me. Yet many churches expend little energy teaching us *why it matters so much*. So what do I deeply *long* for people like my friend to understand?

Seeking and Savoring

Worship isn't just another activity on a smorgasbord of activities Christians have to pick and choose from—and therefore okay to ignore. Because . . .

1) God *commands* us to worship Him.

> *"YOU SHALL WORSHIP THE LORD YOUR GOD, AND SERVE HIM ONLY" (Matthew 4:10).*

And remember, *"He who has My commandments and keeps them is the one who loves Me" (John 14:21a).*

2) God *deserves* our worship.

> *"Great is the LORD and most worthy of praise; His greatness no one can fathom" (Psalm 145:3, NIV).*

3) God's *purpose for us* is to be His worshipers.

> ***"For this reason** also, God highly exalted Him, and bestowed on Him the name which is above every name, **so that** at the name of Jesus EVERY KNEE WILL BOW, of those who are in heaven and on earth and under the earth, and that every tongue will confess that Jesus Christ is Lord, . . ." (Philippians 2:9-11).*

4) God *wired us to grow in transforming intimacy with Himself and in the maturity of our faith* through our worship.

> *"O God, You are my God; . . . I will bless You as long as I live; I will lift up my hands in Your name. My soul is satisfied as with marrow and fatness, And my mouth offers praises with joyful lips" (Psalm 63:1-5).*

Apathy

5) God *wired the Church to grow and thrive* as a result of their worship together.

> *"Let them give thanks to the* LORD *for His lovingkindness, And for His wonders to the sons of men! Let them extol Him also in the congregation of the people, And praise Him at the seat of the elders"* (Psalm 107:31-32).

6) God's *glory reflected to the world* is at stake.

> *"Give praise to the* LORD, *proclaim his name; make known among the nations what he has done"* (Psalm 105:1, NIV).

7) Satan hates the worship of God (for all those reasons) and whispers lies constantly in an attempt to stop us!

[e.g., "God doesn't need it." "It's not important." "It's too hard." "Mouthing the words is enough." "*This other thing* deserves your time and attention more."]

> *"Again, the devil took Him* [Jesus] *to a very high mountain and showed Him all the kingdoms of the world and their glory; and he said to Him, " 'All these things I will give You, if You fall down and worship me.' Then Jesus said to him, 'Go, Satan! For it is written, "YOU SHALL WORSHIP THE LORD YOUR GOD, AND SERVE HIM ONLY." ' "* (Matthew 4:8-10).

Whether it's the product of a cold heart or just pure biblical ignorance on the topic of worship, do you see why God wants us to fight worship apathy? Fight for His glory? What's the solution? This prayer:

"O send out Your light and Your truth, let them lead me; Let them bring me to Your holy hill and to Your dwelling places. Then I will go to the altar of God, to God my exceeding joy; And upon the lyre I shall praise You, O God, my God" (Psalm 43:3-4)!

Reflect

Do I know someone who doesn't enjoy worship? Which of these points do I believe is most misunderstood or disregarded? How is God leading me to respond to these points or verses in regards to my personal worship life?

Respond

Lord God, I praise You that You are worthy of all the worship we could possibly offer You. And I thank You for Your patience as I grow to understand Your desire for me as Your worshiper. Show any place in my heart or mind that is apathetic towards worshiping You or where I'm harboring wrong assumptions or cold traditions. Teach me how to fight for Your glory. . . . <continue>

DAY THIRTY
Near

One day, this statement I heard gripped me: "When I see the cross, . . . I see a God who wasn't content with being distant and detached, but a God who loved us enough to come near."*

And then my heart sank with my very next thought — *and how many people even give a rip?*

The lengths our God went to to "come near" were beyond extraordinary — extraordinarily loving and extraordinarily sacrificial. Yet how many people *bother* to draw *near* to Him in *response?* How many people acknowledge the incredible sacrifice He made so we might even have the *privilege of nearness and intimacy* with God?

I know — life's busy. It's too much work. After all, *He* understands. So we're content with *distant*. And we've grown accustomed to *detached*.

How heartbreaking it must be for God to watch His created ones, especially His *children*, fail to see Him for *who He is* AND for the *intimate relationship* He so *longs* to have with us! The relationship He desires with us is as far in the opposite direction from *distant* as you can get. We can't begin to fathom it. His love is completely overwhelming and His Spirit all-consuming. The only thing we should feel *detached* from is darkness and its allies!

Friend, let's *hear* and *heed* His own words to us, *"Be still and know that I am God! (Psalm 46:10)*. For in that *stillness*—where we grow to *really know Him* (and oh, how God *loves* revealing Himself!)—our desire to draw *near* to Him only increases more and more with each glimpse.

And we have this incredible promise from James, *"Draw near to God and He will draw near to you" (James 4:8)*.

Our God relishes those moments when we stop to commune with Him — to be in His Word, listen to His heart, share what's on ours, and bow in humble worship. And what we *reap* from that sacrifice of time, attention, and focus is *indescribable* and *invaluable*.

Here's a glimpse into the heart of some psalmists who truly loved to bask in the nearness of God:

> *"How lovely are Your dwelling places, O Lord of hosts! My soul longed and even yearned for the courts of the Lord; My heart and my flesh sing for joy to the living God. . . . How blessed are those who dwell in Your house! They are ever praising You. . . . For a day in Your courts is better than a thousand outside. I would rather stand at the threshold of the house of my God than dwell in the tents of wickedness. For the Lord God is a sun and shield; The Lord gives grace and glory; No good thing does He withhold from those who walk uprightly. O Lord of hosts,*

How blessed is the man who trusts in You!" (Psalm 84:1-2, 4; 10-12).

"How blessed is the one whom You choose and bring near to You, To dwell in Your courts. We will be satisfied with the goodness of Your house, Your holy temple" (Psalm 65:4).

"But as for me, the nearness of God is my good" (Psalm 73:28a).

God isn't content with distant and detached, and we shouldn't be either. So *reject* it. *Reject* the lies that say our glances God's way are enough or that it doesn't really matter anyway.

Let what Jesus *did*—from leaving His perfect heaven so he could humbly come to earth as a human baby *to* His torturous death on the cross **just so He could draw us near from now to all eternity**—*drive us to His feet often*. There is so much He longs to do *in* us and *for* us in that place of nearness.

And then humbly respond in *worship*.

Reflect

Have I ever been content with distant and detached in my walk with God? Do I struggle to draw near to God now, or does it come easily? What can I do to grow in my sacrifice of time, attention, and focus in my time with God? How can I let that feed my time savoring my God in worship?

Respond

Lord God, thank You for not being content with distant and detached from me. I worship You, Jesus, for Your overwhelming love and the power of Your Spirit that woos me into Your presence. I praise You for the goodness and blessings You pour out for me there. Help me to thirst for nearness with You. Help me to comprehend how vital that nearness is to my everyday relationship and walk with You. . . . <continue>

*Michelle Cushatt interview

DAY THIRTY-ONE
Church
(part 1)

I found myself riveted on Psalm 95 one morning. Even though the Bible has far more examples of *personal* worship than it does worshiping together as a body of believers, the writer of this psalm has some powerful words about being a worshiping church. I love his *hows* and *whys*, as well as his *warnings*.

Psalm 95:1-7 begins,

> *"O come, let us sing for joy to the LORD, Let us shout joyfully to the rock of our salvation, Let us come before His presence with thanksgiving, Let us shout joyfully to Him with psalms. For the LORD is a great God And a great King above all gods, In whose hand are the depths of the earth, The peaks of the mountains are His also. The sea is His, for it was He who made it, And His hands formed the dry land. Come, let us worship and bow down, Let us kneel before the LORD our Maker. For He is our God, And we are the people of His pasture and the sheep of His hand."*

According to this psalm — as we enter worship together, we must:

1) Employ our will.

"O come." You can show up to church every week and still not *"come"* to worship. In fact, you can engage your voice in singing the songs for others to hear (i.e., *praise*), and still not engage your *will* in *worshiping* – *"sing . . . to the* LORD.*"* So it's important that we respond from deep within our souls to the invitation to *"come"* – each *individual* heart surrendered, yet lifting His name *together* to *Him.* For *His* ears. *"Come, let us sing . . . to the* LORD*!"*

2) Engage our emotions.

We don't just *"sing"* – we *"sing for joy!"* Beyond employing our *will*, we must engage our *emotions* as well. In fact, the original Hebrew word, *nariah*, used for *"sing for joy"* and *"shout joyfully" (vv. 1-2)* expresses the *highest* kind of joy! That's right, the absolute *greatest joy* is called for as we *come* before God – remembering who He is and pouring out ourselves before Him in worship! *" . . . let us sing for [the highest] joy to the* LORD*!"*

3) Apply our minds.

This *joy* isn't just some worked-up emotion. It's the result of *remembering* and *engaging* with the *"rock of our salvation."* It's the aftereffect of declaring, *"the* LORD *is a great God And a King above all gods." "In [His] hand are the depths of the earth, . . . The peaks of the mountains, . . . The sea . . . , He made it!"* It's the intrinsic *why*. Worship is the acknowledging and lifting of *infinite truths* about who God is. Which means, we must . . .

Church (part 1)

4) Know our God.

The many *whys* the psalmist poured out to invite us to worship all had to do with *who God is*. Now, the mind-mouthing *facts* about God can never replace *experientially knowing* our Savior. So we want the type of knowledge that *results in* awe-inspired, utter devotion to Him *expressed* in worship.

The psalmist obviously had very specific personal experiences or events in mind as he wrote each line—covering God's power, goodness, and even gentleness. *"For the LORD is a great God!" "We are . . . [His] sheep."* So besides coming as a body of believers, it's *deeply personal*. I come to worship *my* God—who is *our* God—with *you!*

5) Expect His presence.

God wants us to *expect* to engage with Him *closely* as we lift up our hearts and minds in response to all that He is in worship. He doesn't invite us to worship Him at a *distance*, He longs for us to *draw close*. *"Let us come **before His presence** . . ."* Can you picture it? What grace! We can stand before the King together!

6) Give Him thanks.

Thanksgiving is a necessary ingredient for our heart to be rightly positioned to worship. As this psalmist said, *"Let us come before His presence **with thanksgiving**."* We need to approach God's throne not just remembering, but being *thankful* that He's *"the Rock of our salvation," "a great King above all gods,"* and *the Creator of all we see*. Who is He to you? Come with *thanksgiving*.

Seeking and Savoring

We'll continue this discussion on Psalm 95, but stop to consider these six points first.

Reflect

What stands out to me in this psalm so far as most surprising, challenging, or encouraging? Which of these points is the biggest struggle for me—and why? What is God leading me to grow in regarding worship with my church body?

Respond

Lord God, thank You for this psalm that so beautifully calls the Church to worship You. I worship You for the promise of Your presence as we come. Open my eyes to Your desires, not only for my church, but also for me as part of that body of believers. Show me how to prepare to "come," how to engage when I "come," and what to "expect," when we come together to worship You. . . .
<continue>

DAY THIRTY-TWO
Church

(part 2)

Before we dig further into being a worshiping church from Psalm 95, here's what we've learned so far: We're called to employ our will, engage our emotions, apply our minds, know our God, expect His presence, and give Him thanks. And there's more!

Here's the psalm again:

> "O come, let us sing for joy to the Lord, Let us shout joyfully to the rock of our salvation, Let us come before His presence with thanksgiving, Let us shout joyfully to Him with psalms. For the Lord is a great God And a great King above all gods, In whose hand are the depths of the earth, The peaks of the mountains are His also. The sea is His, for it was He who made it, And His hands formed the dry land. Come, let us worship and bow down, Let us kneel before the Lord our Maker. For He is our God, And we are the people of His pasture and the sheep of His hand" (vv. 1-7).

Seeking and Savoring

We're also called to:

7) Surrender our all.

We shouldn't *limit* the surrender of our mind, emotions, and will. We need to surrender *all*. And that includes having a *physical posture* that's yielded to the Holy Spirit's direction. *"Come, let us worship and **bow down**. Let us **kneel before the** L*ORD *our Maker."*

Many biblical Hebrew and Greek words for worship express there is absolutely nothing passive about the act of worship. Our bowed knees and raised hands are physical expressions of surrendered *hearts* — hearts offering from the deepest depths. So we need to consider how to surrender *all* of who *"our Maker"* created us to be in our worship of Him *as* His Spirit leads. Because He deserves nothing less.

Then, the psalmist suddenly hit the brakes on his worship invitation and felt the need to issue a *warning*:

> *"Today, if you would hear His voice, Do not harden your hearts, as at Meribah, As in the day of Massah in the wilderness, When your fathers tested Me, They tried Me, though they had seen My work. For forty years I loathed [that] generation, And said they are a people who err in their heart, And they do not know My ways"* (vv. 7b-10).

He's warning us, *Church, in order to enter worship together, we must:*

Church (part 2)

8) Guard our hearts.

We need to guard against *"hardened hearts"* and *unbelief*. This psalmist's warning specifically refers to the Israelites' attitudes in Exodus and Numbers. They didn't think God was fulfilling His promises, so doubted who He was. They questioned, *"Is the Lord among us, or not?" (Exodus 17:7)*. They didn't *"hear His voice,"* but doubted His presence. They *"err[ed] in their hearts."* The psalmist is obviously warning us not to repeat Israel's unbelief and sin!

Psalm 95 is later quoted in Hebrews 3, and is followed by,

> *"Take care, brethren, that there not be in any one of you an evil, unbelieving heart that falls away from the living God. But encourage one another day after day, as long as it is still called 'Today,' so that none of you will be hardened by the deceitfulness of sin" (vv. 12-13).*

True worship comes from hearts that are in a right relationship with God. Otherwise,

> *" '... this people draw near with their words and honor Me with their lip service, But they remove their hearts far from Me, and their reverence for Me consists of tradition learned by rote' " (Isaiah 29:13).*

So learning from all of these verses, may we be ready to *"come"* together to worship — *"singing for [the highest] joy"* to our God *"with thanksgiving"* as we proclaim who He is. May we not doubt *"His presence,"* but *"hear His*

Seeking and Savoring

voice." May we not engage *in part*, but come surrendering *all*. And may we *"encourage one another day after day"* (important!), so we don't *"harden"* or *"err in [our] hearts."*

Church, let's come *ready to intimately engage* our God together! Because *"the* LORD *is a great God!" "He is **our** God!"* It's an unspeakable taste of His mercy and grace and the greatest privilege on this earth. Let's be a *worshiping Church!*

> *"For this reason also, God highly exalted Him, and bestowed on Him the name which is above every name, so that at the name of Jesus every knee will bow, of those who are in heaven and on earth and under the earth, and that every tongue will confess that Jesus Christ is Lord, to the glory of God the Father" (Philippians 2:9-11).*

Reflect

How do these final two points from Psalm 95 challenge or encourage me? How do I feel God calling me to respond to the challenges in this psalm regarding my corporate worship?

Respond

Lord God, thank You for calling Your church together to worship You. I praise You for being the only true, worthy

Church (part 2)

God. Help me to guard my heart against unbelief and hardness so I am always ready to approach Your throne to intimately worship You. Remind me to be an encouragement to others in their walks with You and worship of You. May we always come surrendering our all at Your feet. . . . <continue>

DAY THIRTY-THREE
Names

The importance of names is abundantly clear in the Bible. As much as I enjoy and am blessed by all of *my* names and the roles they call me into—Pam, Mom, Memaw, and more—God's many names are *so much more important*. God reveals His names to us in the Bible to display *exactly* who He is and *all* His character holds. It's an important part of *knowing* God and worshiping *all* that He is. Plus, His Word tells us that He wants us to *remember* His name, *call* on His name, and *exalt* His name. And while He performed many mighty deeds *in response to* people calling upon His name (read 1 Kings 18:21-39 for one of those amazing stories), there are also accounts of what happened to those who forgot His name. (Read a not-so-amazing story in Jeremiah 23:25-27.)

Here are some of God's directives to *remember, call on,* and *exalt* His name:

> **"I am the Lord, that is My name; I will not give My glory to another, Nor My praise to graven images"** (Isaiah 42:8).

> *"Some boast in chariots and some in horses, But* **we will boast in the name of the Lord, our God"** (Psalm 20:7).

Names

*"Help us, O God of our salvation, **for the glory of Your name**; And deliver us and forgive our sins **for Your name's sake**" (Psalm 79:9).*

"It is good to give thanks to the LORD *And to **sing praises to Your name, O Most High**" (Psalm 92:1).*

*"**O** LORD**, I remember Your name in the night**, And keep Your law" (Psalm 119:55).*

*"I will bow down toward Your holy temple And **give thanks to Your name** for Your lovingkindness and Your truth; For **You have magnified Your word according to all Your name**" (Psalm 138:2).*

*"Pray, then, in this way: 'Our Father who is in heaven, **Hallowed be Your name**' " (Matthew 6:9).*

*"AND IT SHALL BE THAT **EVERYONE WHO CALLS ON THE NAME OF THE LORD WILL BE SAVED**" (Acts 2:21).*

I've been really challenged by this recently. It's motivated me to better know and specifically exalt God's names. And it's reminded me of the *power* in each of His names.

Think about it. He has each of those names because He *is* each of those names. Besides experiencing tremendous awe at each remembrance of His name, we should also experience incredible joy, hope, strength, comfort, confidence, and many other things as we stop to call out to and proclaim our God. The power of each of His names stirs and confirms in us a truth that is truly transforming. And the entirety of His Word only confirms all that His name is in every way. I've decided that I want His names on the tip of my tongue for whenever I need to call on them, and so I can adore and humble myself before those names in worship. Because He wants me to have no doubt about *who He is*. He wants the same for you.

[I've included a list of the names, titles, and descriptions of God in the back of this book. Use it frequently to guide your times of seeking and worshiping Him.]

Reflect

Do I ever use God's names in my times of prayer and worship? What benefits do I see in learning and using them more? How do these verses encourage my use of God's names? What steps should I take to grow in my knowledge, understanding, and use of God's names?

Respond

Almighty God, I worship You for the greatness and power of Your great name. I thank You that You long for me to know and worship all that You are. I pray that You would help me to grow in my knowledge of You and Your names so I might worship You more fully. Remind me

Names

often of the power of each of Your names so I might be transformed by who You are. I worship You right here and now for being. . . . <continue, referring to list of names>

DAY THIRTY-FOUR
Jehoshaphat

It doesn't take a theologian or psychologist to tell us life is a series of battles—large and small, from with*in* and with*out*. So I love the story of King Jehoshaphat and the people of Judah in 2 Chronicles 20:1-24. For it's a story of bowed-down, battle-bracing *worship* in the midst of enormous battle!

The story begins with Jehoshaphat getting word that *"a great multitude"* was on their way to *"make war"* against them. And the first thing he did was *acknowledge his fear*, *seek God*, and *proclaim a fast* throughout Judah. *And* the people united! (It's hard to not point out what most kings would have done—call together an army!) Now, King Jehoshaphat has got all of Judah together—specifically, *"All the men of Judah, with their wives and children and little ones, stood there before the Lord" (v. 13).* (Is your heart in your throat yet?) And he called upon God, saying,

> "'O Lord, *the God of our fathers,* **are You not** *God in the heavens? And are You not ruler over all the kingdoms of the nations? Power and might are in Your hand so that no one can stand against You.* **'Did You not**, *O our God, drive out the inhabitants of this land before Your people Israel and give it to the descendants of Abraham Your friend forever? . . . we* **are powerless** *before this great multitude who are*

coming against us; **nor do we know what to do, but our eyes are on You***"* *(vv .6-7, 12).*

Jehoshaphat began his prayer by acknowledging *who God was* and proclaiming His *power* and *might.* He worshiped! He then continued by *restating* God's promises, *recounting* God's past faithfulness, and *admitting* his own powerlessness and lack of wisdom. He boldly proclaimed his trust in God as he and Judah sought the Lord together in this time of crisis. *Many* lessons for us there!

Then God's Spirit sent word through a prophet, *"the battle is not yours, but God's,"* and gave instructions on what to do next.

"'You will not have to fight this battle. Take up your positions; stand firm and see the deliverance the Lord will give you, Judah and Jerusalem. Do not be afraid; do not be discouraged. **Go out to face them** *tomorrow, and the Lord will be with you'" (vv. 14-17).*

Then they surely came up with a backup plan in case this plan failed. They didn't? Instead, *"Jehoshaphat bowed down with his face to the ground, and all the people of Judah and Jerusalem fell down in* **worship** *before the Lord" (v. 18).*

What a powerful message and response. God says, *"Do not fear. Trust Me."* And their quick reply, *"We trust You. We worship You."*

Seeking and Savoring

Just think—impending war, "go out, but don't fight," with little ones in their arms—and let their response sink in for a minute.

The next morning, Jehoshaphat stood before Judah again, and said, "*Listen to me, Judah and people of Jerusalem! Have faith in the Lord your God and you will be upheld*" (v. 20). As if we didn't have *enough* reason to be impressed by their faith already, then *this* happened:

> "*After consulting the people,* **Jehoshaphat appointed men to sing to the Lord and to praise him for the splendor of his holiness** *as they went out at the head of the army, saying: 'Give thanks to the Lord, for his **love** endures forever'* " (v. 21).

(Ok, I've sung on a lot of worship teams, but I can totally see myself passing on this offer!)

Of course, "*as they began to sing and praise, the Lord set ambushes against the men of Ammon and Moab and Mount Seir who were invading Judah, and they were defeated. . . . [the enemy] helped to destroy one another. . . . no one had escaped*" (vv. 22-24).

Only. God. But *don't move on too quickly*—keep processing this for a minute.

Receiving instructions and *following through* with them are two *very* different things. They stepped out in faith and trusted God before *any* physical signs of an answer. There would have been *so many* barriers to standing weaponless in front of a multitude of warriors like that—like fear, faithlessness, and helplessness. But

Jehoshaphat

Jehoshaphat reminded his people to *put their trust in the Lord and succeed*. And then the appointed worshipers lifted their voices to declare *the lovingkindness of the Lord!* They weren't singing about God's strength and might— but about His everlasting *love!*

God knows that **Satan fears the worship of God most of all.** So when Judah went out before the army and proclaimed God's *lovingkindness*, there *couldn't* have been a more devastating assault on the approaching enemy! The power of *faith-filled worship* is exhibited in an amazing way in this moment! And there is a great lesson for us in that.

Reflect

What if I acknowledged who God was and worshiped Him as a *first* step when facing battles? What if we were more bold to worship God together as we face battles in life? Could God be waiting to do things on my behalf (even on a smaller scale) that I miss out on, because I don't stop to acknowledge or worship Him first? What did I learn about being a true worshiper from this story?

Seeking and Savoring

Respond

Lord God, I praise You that power and might are in Your hands and You rule over all! I praise You that I can call on You in any situation and You hear my cries — You are always here with me. May I see and hope in Your lovingkindness in every situation life throws my way. Remind me to remember, acknowledge, and worship You first — always. . . . <continue>

*This devotion includes excerpts from my book, *Worship and the Word*.

DAY THIRTY-FIVE
Overwhelmed

Do you remember the last time you felt overwhelmed? I do. And it's embarrassing what led to those overwhelmed feelings. Nothing life-threatening in the least. Nothing even remotely bad. I just let something get the best of me.

*Until I sensed God saying to me, Pam, you're overwhelmed by these things, because you're not overwhelmed by **Me** right now. Get back to that place of being overwhelmed by **who I am** — for you, in you, and through you.*

And that reminded me of Jesus' words to His friend,

> " 'Martha, Martha, you are worried and bothered about so many things; but only one thing is necessary, for Mary has chosen the good part, which shall not be taken away from her' " (Luke 10:41-42). (And we remember what Mary chose.)

It was time to take a deep breath and refocus on *Him who should overwhelm me completely.*

Every pore of our being needs to be overwhelmed by our God and the truth of all that He is. Otherwise when those stressful times blindside us, all of the dry, cracked, weary, God-thirsty space inside us will quickly become overwhelmed by all of the wrong things instead.

The truth is — *the center of my focus will always get the best of me.* (Read that again.)

If I'm diligent to make sure that my focus stays on *God*, then He will constantly give me *way more* of His overwhelmingly indescribable self and His promises to dwarf any situation in comparison. It puts everything in perspective according to *who He is.*

And I know my God well enough to know that even in those times of my life when I've been overwhelmed by *much greater* life-altering situations, He has *always* provided the hope, peace, wisdom, and victory that I so desperately needed. He is always faithful. Always loving. Always here.

> *"Why are you in despair, O my soul? And why have you become disturbed within me? Hope in God, for I shall again praise Him for the help of His presence"* (Psalm 42:5).

And worship? Being overwhelmed by God needs to be my priority so that I will live a life that never fails to worship Him — both on my knees and in how I live my life. Being overwhelmed by God *propels* me into a life of worshiping Him!

Not there yet? That's okay. Ask God to *reveal* more of Himself to you and to help you wait, see, and *respond* with your whole being. He loves answering those prayers.

Overwhelmed

Reflect

When was the last time I felt overwhelmed, and how did I deal with it? How have I seen the center of my focus getting the best of me—good or bad? What steps should I take to be more overwhelmed by God than by life around me?

Respond

Lord God, I thank and praise You that You are far greater than any situation life could throw my way. I love and worship You for the hope, peace, wisdom, and victory You graciously pour out on me as I seek You. Help me to be overwhelmed by who You are for me at all times. Help me to wait, see, and respond to You with my whole being in worship. . . . <continue>

DAY THIRTY-SIX
Unreasonable

I was on my knees one day about to approach God in worship, and it hit me: *This is so unreasonable! It makes no sense to this brain of mine that I should be able to do this!*

What's so unreasonable?

1. It's unreasonable that a holy, Almighty God would allow lowly me in His *presence*. Because . . .

> *"For who in the skies is comparable to the* L ORD*? Who among the sons of the mighty is like the* L ORD*, a God greatly feared in the council of the holy ones, and awesome above all those who are around Him? O* L ORD *God of hosts, who is like You, O mighty* L ORD*?" (Psalm 89:6-8a).*

Except . . . *"But as for me,* **by Your abundant lovingkindness I will enter Your house***, At Your holy temple I will bow in reverence for You" (Psalm 5:7).*

"How blessed is the one **whom You choose and bring near to You***, To dwell in Your courts. We will be satisfied with the goodness of Your house, Your holy temple" (Psalm 65:4).*

Unreasonable

2. It's unreasonable that God would *want* to *commune* with me here. Because . . .

> *"When I consider Your heavens, the work of Your fingers, The moon and the stars, which You have ordained; What is man that You take thought of him, And the son of man that You care for him?" (Psalm 8:3-4).*

Except . . . *"How precious also are Your thoughts to me, O God! How vast is the sum of them!" (Psalm 139:17).*

" . . . the LORD *is with you when you are with Him. And if you seek Him, He will let you find Him" (2 Chronicles 15:2).*

3. It's unreasonable that God would choose to *reveal* Himself to me. Because . . .

Just as John said of Jesus, " . . . *the sandals of whose feet I am not worthy to untie" (Acts 13:25).*

Except . . . *"This is eternal life, that they know You, the only true God, and Jesus Christ, whom You have sent" (John 17:3).*

> *"All things have been handed over to Me by My Father; and no one knows the Son except the Father; nor does anyone know the Father except the Son, and* **anyone to whom the Son wills to reveal Him"** *(Matthew 11:27).*

Seeking and Savoring

4. It's unreasonable to think that I could have *anything worthy to offer my God* in worship. Because . . .

> *"For all have sinned and fall short of the glory of God,"* *(Romans 3:23).*

Except . . . *"Now to Him who is able to keep you from stumbling, and **to make you stand in the presence of His glory blameless** with great joy, to the only God our Savior, **through Jesus Christ our Lord**, be glory, majesty, dominion and authority, before all time and now and forever. Amen"* *(Jude 1:24-25).*

> *"For we do not have a high priest who cannot **sympathize with our weaknesses**, but One who has been tempted in all things as we are, yet without sin. Therefore let us **draw near with confidence to the throne of grace**, so that we may receive mercy and find grace to help in time of need"* *(Hebrews 4:16).*

Worship is so *unreasonable* from a mere human perspective! God's *love* is unreasonable. His *forgiveness* is unreasonable. His *grace* and *faithfulness* are unreasonable.

Except they are the absolute *truest* things in our lives.

Except Jesus paid the penalty for our sins *for no other reason than His unfathomable love would have it no other way.*

So that we could worship Him. It's His plan.

Unreasonable

> *"**For this reason** also, God highly exalted Him, and bestowed on Him the name which is above every name, **so that at the name of Jesus every knee will bow**, of those who are in heaven and on earth and under the earth, and that every tongue will confess that Jesus Christ is Lord, to the glory of God the Father"* (Philippians 2:9-11).

May we never forget how *unreasonable* it is that we are allowed to worship at the throne of the Creator God of the universe. And may we never forget *the only reason why* the humble privilege is ours. Jesus.

> *"Not to us, O Lord, not to us but to your name be the glory, **because of your love and faithfulness**"* (Psalm 115:1, NIV).

Reflect

What do I find the most unreasonable about worship? How do these verses that express the lengths God has gone to so we might worship Him impact how I view God and my worship of Him?

Seeking and Savoring

Respond

My God, thank You for Your unreasonable, unfathomable love. I thank and praise You for Your faithfulness and grace toward me. I thank You that You long to commune with me and reveal Yourself to me as I worship. Help me never forget what Jesus did so I might have a relationship with You here on earth and for all eternity. . . . <continue>

DAY THIRTY-SEVEN
Adore

*Oh come, **let us adore Him**, Oh come, let us adore Him, Oh come, let us adore Him, Christ the Lord.*

We sing it over and over every Christmas, but do we pay attention to what it means? Do we accept the invitation all year long?

Like most songs we repeat throughout our life, I think it's easy to sing the words without much thought. But we really can't afford to miss out on what's called for here—*adoration*—for it's one of the foundational elements of worship.

Though the word, *adoration*, never occurs in our English language Bibles, the act of adoring God is definitely present in the Bible. The word is derived from Latin *adorare*, meaning, to express honor or reverence, from the Latin root, *os (oris)*, meaning, mouth. It's the picture of kissing your hand to then express extreme devotion toward another.

But why is adoration something that so many of us struggle to actually express towards God?

A kiss is merely an empty action unless it originates in the heart. In Luke 6:45, Jesus says that the *"mouth*

Seeking and Savoring

speaks from that which fills his heart." So to engage in true worship, we must *first* have hearts that are *full of love and adoration for our God*. Of course, this only happens, as in any relationship, by spending time with Him—communing with Him, asking Him to reveal Himself to us, and filling our minds with His truth. *Then* we'll be so full of love for Him that we won't *merely* lift our voices and hands in worship, but we'll *first* lift our hearts.

> *"Praise the* Lord*. I will extol the* Lord ***with all my heart*** *in the council of the upright and in the assembly" (Psalm 111:1, NIV).*

I know this can be a confusing or even frustrating topic—when it might seem like we're just trying to add emotions to worship. I know some people reveal little to no emotion during worship, while others seem to have it in abundance. And there are times you may feel moved more strongly than others. But this has *nothing* to do with emotions for the sake of emotions, and *everything* to do with **hearts *fully surrendered and responding* to the God who *first* poured out His heart for us.**

Because it's Jesus who said, " **'Love the Lord your God with all your heart** *and with all your soul and with all your mind' " (Matthew 22:36-37, NIV).*

And David gave us these pictures of his adoring heart during worship:

> *"Teach me Your way, O* Lord*; I will walk in Your truth;* ***Unite my heart*** *to fear Your name. I will give thanks to You, O Lord my God,* ***with all my***

heart, *And will glorify Your name forever"* (Psalm 86:11-12).

*"I will praise you, L*ORD*, **with all my heart**; I will tell of all the marvelous things you have done"* (Psalm 9:1, NLT).

God would love to answer a prayer like this: *God, help me to respond to You in worship with all I am. Help me to get past the distractions and noise to see You, know You, and **adore** You. Help me to guard my heart so it's completely Yours. For You are completely worthy of all my heart could ever offer You.*

So *come*, let us *adore* Him! With *all our heart*—for He alone is worthy! Jesus Christ the Lord!

Reflect

How do I picture adoration in regards to worship? Do I struggle to feel or express emotions during worship—even internally? What steps do I feel God is asking me to take to grow in my adoration of Him?

Respond

Oh, God, I thank and praise You for being completely worthy of my worship and surrendered heart. May this heart and mind of mine be so filled with the knowledge and love of You that I can't help but surrender all to You in worship. May I always allow Your Holy Spirit to guide my time at Your throne so it's a fragrant aroma to You.... <continue>

DAY THIRTY-EIGHT
Stop

I don't like what we've allowed our changing world to do to us. We live in a time when we have to fight really hard to have focus, attention, and contemplation—even if we *don't* have ADD. So is it any wonder that the God who created us *firmly* and *lovingly* says, *"Be still."* Not just physically, but we must fight to still the mind and soul as well. Why? In order to *"know that I am God"* (Psalm 46:10).

I think He knows us pretty well. He knows in order for us to really *see* Him and *hear* Him, stillness is required. The kind of stillness that asks, *"What do You want to tell me?" "What do You want to show me?"* or says, *"Help me to know You more in this moment, Jesus."*

God even placed us in this amazing world He created to bring *Himself* glory and to constantly *reveal Himself* to us. So much so, Paul said man is *"without excuse,"* because what is *"known about God is evident"* and *"clearly seen"* in His spectacular creation (Romans 1:19-20).

Yet frankly, I think even those of us who *believe* with all our hearts far too easily overlook it. And therefore overlook *Him* in it. I know I'm guilty.

Seeking and Savoring

What are we missing when we *don't* stop? When we're not *still* enough to take in what He's revealing in the moment? The story of His faithfulness, His power, and His wisdom? Or maybe it's His creativity, impeccable attention to detail, and even sense of humor. Or how about *His love*? Obviously, it's all those things and *so much more* than we can possibly imagine!

Here's what various psalmists observed:

> "The heavens are telling of the **glory of God**; And their expanse is declaring the work of His hands. Day to day pours forth speech, And night to night reveals **knowledge**" (Psalm 19:1-2).

> "The heavens declare **His righteousness**, And all the peoples have seen **His glory**" (Psalm 97:6).

> "When I consider Your heavens, the work of Your fingers, The moon and the stars, which You have ordained; What is man that **You take thought of him**, And the son of man that **You care for him?**" (Psalm 8:3-4).

> "[Give thanks] To Him who made the heavens with skill,
> **For His lovingkindness is everlasting;**
> To Him who spread out the earth above the waters,
> **For His lovingkindness is everlasting;**
> To Him who made the great lights,
> **For His lovingkindness is everlasting:**
> The sun to rule by day,
> **For His lovingkindness is everlasting,**
> The moon and stars to rule by night,

Stop

For His lovingkindness is everlasting" (Psalm 136:5-9).

I don't know about you, but I need to *stop* more. Dead still. And I need to take in all He's trying to tell me about Himself. I hate to think how much I've missed out on already, because I simply wasn't paying attention. And I hate to think how my view of God and the depths of my worship have suffered, because I missed a revealing moment.

I think if we begin our day by asking God to open our eyes to all He wants us to see, He'd love to oblige. Taking time to *stop* – while praying, reading His Word, or taking in life around us – is one of the good habits that can *breathe new life* into our worship.

I love the passage in Isaiah 41 that explains how God will answer the afflicted and needy. He said He'll provide various flowing waters (v. 18) and many kinds of trees (v. 19) **so that** *"they may see and recognize, and consider and gain insight as well, that the hand of the* LORD *has done this, and the Holy One of Israel has created it." Isaiah 41:20*

I love that progression:

See → Recognize → Consider → Gain insight

Each one is a step further into the commitment to *stop* – and not merely glance. Once we *"see,"* if we don't then do the double take to *"recognize,"* and pause further to *"consider,"* then we don't *"gain* [new] *insight"* into our God.

Seeking and Savoring

Commit with me to *stop* more. Let's ask Him for eyes to gain new insights into who He is, so we might see that indeed *"the hand of the LORD has done this."* And worship Him.

Reflect

When have I had a powerful moment with God when I decided to *stop*? Do I need to stop more often? What should I do to discipline myself to stop more?

Respond

Lord God, thank You for revealing Yourself in everything I see in creation and for how it all reveals Your glory, righteousness, lovingkindness, and grace. I praise You for the lengths You've gone to to draw me closer. Help me to remember to stop more often. Open my eyes so I might take in all You're trying to tell me about Yourself. Open my eyes to Your hand at work. . . . <continue>

DAY THIRTY-NINE
Flip

How seriously do I take distractions from my worship of God? Do they really matter?

Jesus took distractions from worship seriously. We know this from reading Matthew 21:12-13 (NIV): *"Jesus entered the temple courts and drove out all who were buying and selling there. He overturned the tables of the money-changers and the benches of those selling doves. 'It is written,' he said to them, 'My house will be called a house of prayer, but you are making it a den of robbers.' "*

What were they robbing? Not only were they deceitfully taking people's money, they were also robbing Gentiles of their dedicated, undistracted place of worship and prayer in the outer courts of the temple. Jesus had made it clear three years prior this was an unacceptable practice (John 2:14-16). But their businesses, even under the guise of being religious, were still inhibiting worship. *Their* priority was the monetary gain of worldly business. *Jesus'* priority was the soulful gain of anyone who would choose to come and worship the Father there.

While we don't sell doves and exchange currency in churches these days, we do often have things in our lives and churches that inhibit ourselves, and others around us, from worshiping God. We have *tables*, so to speak, that desperately need to be flipped.

We need to get rid of anything that weighs us down, distracts us, clutters our minds, or holds us back in any way. We need to remember and diligently fulfill the prerequisites for being true worshipers of the Most High God, such as having *"clean hands and a pure heart" (Psalm 24:3-5)* — instead of believing that going through the religious motions is enough.

Don't forget Mary of Bethany and how she found herself at Jesus' feet regardless of what was going on around her. Regardless of the urgent, the grief, or the criticism, her priority was obvious, and her worship was fathoms deep because of it.

As we flip the worship-robbing tables in our own lives, the worship in our temples will be fueled as never before. After all, *we* are now the *temple*.

> *"Do you not know that you are a temple of God and that the Spirit of God dwells in you?" (1 Corinthians 3:16)*.

Our holy, infinite God lives *in* us! Can you even comprehend it? And that God who lives in us is *wholly deserving* and *worthy* of *all* of our strivings to have a worshiper's *devoted heart*. So let's flip some tables!

Flip

Reflect

Just as Jesus cleaned out the temple so nothing would hinder the worship there, is there anything in me I need to allow Him to clean out or flip over that's inhibiting my worship—at home or church? What can I do to ensure I have approached God in worship without distractions?

Respond

Thank You, God, for being worthy of all the worship I could ever offer You. I thank and praise You for giving me Your Spirit to indwell me to guide and empower my worship. Please open my eyes to anything in my life that is distracting me or inhibiting my worship in any way. Help me to offer You all You deserve at Your throne. . . .
<continue>

DAY FORTY
Snorkel?

Have you ever snorkeled? The beauty that lies just below the ocean's surface is breathtaking. And it always makes me long for *more*—more unknowns, greater depths, unimaginable wonders! Because I know floating on the surface doesn't begin to give me a picture of all that waits for me in the *depths*.

Of course, I rarely have the opportunity to take in the ocean's treasures. But when it comes to the *things of God* (aka *the Creator of all the seas*), we have *no excuse*! We're wired from the moment of salvation through God's Spirit to intimately know God.

> *"Now we have received, not the spirit of the world, but the Spirit who is from God, so that we may know the things freely given to us by God" (1 Corinthians 2:12).*

In fact, we're continually called to *dive deeper* in both our *relationship* with Him and in our *worship intimacy* with Him.

Proverbs 2:3-5 says, *"For **if** you cry for discernment, lift your voice for understanding; **If** you seek her as silver, and search for her as for hidden treasures; **Then** you will discern* *the fear of the* LORD, *and discover the* **knowledge of God**" (bold emphasis mine).

This proverb describes an active pursuit of knowing and understanding God and the things of God. Because, we can't react to what we don't know. **We can only worship God to the degree that we know Him.** Otherwise, it's much like trying to go deep-sea diving with a snorkel. We've heard that so many amazing things lie in the vast waters far beyond what we can see. But if we're only willing to float on the surface of the water with a snorkel, then we can never truly experience or attempt to *know* that vastness. Instead, we *settle* for the *shallowness*.

And the treasures in the shallowness are not even a speck on the expanse of all that lies waiting to be revealed. And that ocean? Well, it's merely a speck on the vastness of all that is waiting to be revealed *of God*. After all, He created it — along with the rest of the universe! But unlike the ocean, God *longs* to reveal Himself to us. He relishes those times we're willing to dive in headfirst and search with great expectancy for what He has for us next. Will it be the greater wonders of His love? His faithfulness? His power? His mercy?

After all, in Romans 11:33, 36 we read, *"Oh, the depth of the riches both of the wisdom and knowledge of God! How unsearchable are His judgments and unfathomable His ways! . . . For from Him and through Him and to Him are all things. To Him be the glory forever. Amen."*

And I love Psalm 43, because the psalmist asks God to *reveal* Himself through His Word and His Spirit and prays his *response* to that revelation would then be to *worship!*

> "O send out Your light and Your truth, let them lead me; Let them bring me to Your holy hill and to Your dwelling places. **Then** I will go to the altar of God, to God my exceeding joy; And upon the lyre I shall praise You, O God, my God" (Psalm 43:3-4).

Do we dive headfirst into our personal times with God—striving determinedly and vigorously against the waters of passivity to know Him more?

What about our worship? Do we come with hearts prepared, minds focused, and souls surrendered? Do we enter His presence with an expectation of diving into the depths to *see* and *respond to* the hidden things God has for us? Because once we've gotten a glimpse of the depths of the glory of God, our compulsion to go back will grow with each new revelation and every taste of intimacy with Him. We'll truly *long* for more!

That's why I spend time in God's Word every day. *And* that's why on my way to church, I ask God to help me offer Him pleasing, acceptable worship that day. I pray against distractions (which are many), and ask that He'd show me anything that might prevent me from worshiping Him fully surrendered. Finally, I ask Him to open the eyes of my heart and mind to whatever He has for me. I don't want to settle for less.

We're each called to so much more than the shallowness of snorkeling our way through worship—than taking *distant glances* at God.

Snorkel?

Make it personal. Ask God's Spirit to help you dive deeper and draw closer. Pray your heart would grow to seek and respond to God in greater ways—for a heart that is impassioned, patient, expectant, and open *as you offer Him all you are in response to all He is*. Because He is worthy!

Reflect

Do I enter worship expecting intimacy with God? Do I strive to dive deeper in my relationship with Him and worship of Him? What steps is God leading me to take to grow in the depths of my worship of Him?

Respond

Thank You, God, for longing to reveal Yourself to me. I praise You for Your light and truth that lead to Your throne to worship You. Help me to draw near to You with a prepared heart and focused mind to dive deep into all You have for me there. Help me to enter worship fully surrendered and with great expectation of Your presence.... <continue>

---

*This devotion includes excerpts from my book, Worship and the Word.

DAY FORTY-ONE
Self

Do you realize how much we're like Adam and Eve? (That's hard to hear, isn't it?)

God created the first man and woman, and then He did that thing He does. *"[He] blessed them"* (Genesis 1:28). He blessed them *abundantly*, in fact! They were handed a barrier-free relationship with their Creator (can you even imagine!), control over all the earth, and all of their needs met *perfectly*—because that's how God rolls. Then He stood back, looked at all He made, and saw it was *very good* (Genesis 1:31). No longer just good, but *very* good.

I really wish there were an "and they all lived happily ever after" at that point in the Bible. But *they. Wanted. More.* <sigh>

Before you put them on your list of people to track down in heaven (admit it, you have one) to ask, "What in the world were you thinking?"—*aren't we the same?*

> *"But I am afraid that, as the serpent deceived Eve by his craftiness, your minds will be led astray from the simplicity and purity of devotion to Christ"* (2 Corinthians 11:3).

Self

Here we are—blessed *"with every spiritual blessing in the heavenly places in Christ" (Ephesians 1:3)*, with *"adoption as sons" (Ephesians 1:5)*, gifted, glorified, forgiven, and free! (And a *whole* lot more!) But like Adam and Eve, *we want more*. We don't want to miss out. We think we know better. We want to feel in charge, important, and unstoppable. Forgetting both *"I can do all things through Him" (Philippians 4:13)* and *"apart from Me you can do nothing" (John 15:5)*, we'd rather rely on *self* than God. And that deception weakens our every move. Worse yet, it prevents our *fellowship with* and *worship of* God.

Have you noticed how many "You can do it!" books and blogs are out there? Not saying that striving to be your best is bad. Not at all. But when self-*encouragement* turns into true self-*sufficiency*, we've lost sight of the God who made us and *placed every single good thing about us* there, not just for our enjoyment, but for *His glory*. *"Let the one who boasts, boast in the Lord" (2 Corinthians 10:17, ESV)*!

His glory. There's an urgent need for Christians to remember who God is and who *we* are *only because of His unfathomable grace and mercy*. We need to *remember* and *thank Him* often.

We need to ask God to show us when we can't get our eyes *off ourselves* long enough to *see Him*. Or when our lives exalt *"me!"* instead of *"He!"* Or when our worship struggles because our view of self is way too *big* (i.e., self-centered, proud) to be *surrendered* before our Creator Savior. Because frankly, there are times when I sing, "There is no other Name," but live like the other name is *mine*. <sigh> (Even when I know the blessings

Seeking and Savoring

He longs to pour out *far exceed* anything else I may be grasping for—fruit or not.)

Let's get out of the way, and *seek Him first. Love* Him first. Let's take the time to make sure our perspective of *who He is* (as well as *self*) is rooted in biblical *truth.* And then by His incredible grace and mercy, *give Him all the glory He deserves* through the power of *His Spirit* at work within us.

He alone deserves that highest place in our lives. Let's fight for *God*-worship in this *self*-loving world.

Reflect

How can I relate to the concept of wanting more than what God has already given me? Do I have a tendency to rely on myself in certain situations rather than finding my sufficiency in Him? What do I need to remember to thank God for more often? How do I need to let that influence my worship of Him?

Respond

Lord God, I thank You for Your patience with me as Your child. Thank You for Your forgiveness when I put myself first and for Your guidance to get me back on track. Help me to get my eyes off of myself so I might see You more clearly. Help to to live a life that glorifies Your name above

Self

all — especially over mine. And help me to seek You first, love You first, and give You all the glory You deserve....
<continue>

DAY FORTY-TWO
Leper

If you want to grow in the depths of your worship, look no further than the measure of your conviction of *who you believe God to be*. This can be backed up by every worshiper of God in the Bible, and that's true for the leper we find in Matthew 8:1-3 as well.

It reads, *"When Jesus came down from the mountain, large crowds followed Him. And a leper came to Him and bowed down before Him, and said, 'Lord, if You are willing, You can make me clean.' Jesus stretched out His hand and touched him, saying, 'I am willing; be cleansed.' And immediately his leprosy was cleansed" (vv. 1-3).*

At first glance, this is a short and simple three-verse story that can be easily overlooked. But one day, I was nudged to check the original Greek word for *"bowed down."* And to my delight, it was a form of *proskeuneo*, a word for *worship,* which specifically means, *to bow and kiss.* This changed how I read this story completely!

So, we've got a man who is forced to live outside of town, forbidden to approach others, required to wear torn clothes and a covering for his mouth, and obligated to cry out *"unclean!"* to all (Leviticus 13:45). *But* after Jesus' Sermon on the Mount, we suddenly find this leper not only defying these laws around this large crowd, but he's also physically and boldly approaching Jesus, bowing at His feet, *and likely* even kissing them! We can only imagine the horror of the surrounding crowd as they watched this scene play out—especially as the leper reached for their newfound Messiah's feet. But instead of pulling back, Jesus responded by compassionately reaching out in return, touching him, and healing this horribly diseased, scorned man. It was a powerful *"Lord, if you are willing. . ." – Yes,"I am willing"* moment.

This leper bowing in worship to Jesus was a display of faith and confidence in who he believed Jesus to be *before* Jesus even had a chance to respond to his faith-filled statement. Would the leper have so boldly approached Jesus had he any doubt of who Jesus was and His ability to heal him? I don't think so. The repercussions would've been harsh. But he expressed his faith through his worship and his words.

It's a beautiful picture of Hebrews 4:16, *"Therefore let us draw near with confidence to the throne of grace, so that we may receive mercy and find grace to help in time of need."* It's a staggering image of how to approach God's throne with *"confidence"* and of the *"mercy"* and *"grace"* we can most certainly find there.

So we have to ask ourselves—do we allow our confidence in who Jesus is to dictate how boldly we approach His throne? Even when others are watching, listening, or even rebuking us? What is God *"willing"* to do on our behalf if we allow unshakeable faith to lead us to His feet? Perhaps He'd respond by reaching out to touch us in return. And perhaps we'd find a greater picture of His mercy and grace.

Seeking and Savoring

As Paul emphasized to the Ephesians, *"In Him and through faith in Him we may enter God's presence with boldness and confidence" (Ephesians 3:12, BSB).*

So seek Him, and He'll let you find Him (Jeremiah 29:13). And then respond boldly and confidently to your merciful, grace-giving God out of your faith-building times with Him in faith-filled worship.

Reflect

How am I moved by this leper's story? Does how I approach God in worship express bold confidence or doubt in who He is? What steps should I take so I might approach God more boldly and confidently?

Respond

My God, thank You that I don't have to doubt who You are — not as I approach You to pray or to worship. I praise You for inviting me to draw near to Your throne with confidence where I know I can find mercy, grace, and love. Help me to allow who I know You to be from Your Word to give me that confidence and guide me in my worship of You. May my faith in You be unshakeable. . . .
<continue>

DAY FORTY-THREE
Wait

We find ourselves waiting for a lot of things—both the important and the not-so-much. And admittedly, sometimes the waiting drudgery goes *on* and *on* ad nauseam.

It was during a period of challenging waiting that God led me to these verses:

> "I **wait** for the LORD, *my soul does wait, And in His word do I hope. My soul **waits** for the Lord **more** than the watchmen for the morning; Indeed, more than the watchmen for the morning*" (Psalm 130:5-6).

After reading it, I paused to consider just *how* the watchmen who wait for the morning *wait*. Because it says I need to wait *"more"* than that! So I thought about how the watchman waits until morning shows up. He waits until the morning shows him what it's come to show him—until it's shone its *light* on the things that it wants him to see. He waits until the morning has *revealed* what's in the dark places. He waits until the morning has *accomplished its purpose* for him. And *then* he can stop waiting—until evening calls again.

It didn't take me long to figure out that not only do I wait for other things more hours of the day than I wait for God, but I also often wait more *thought-consuming, emotion-driven* hours of the day for them—*only* to be let down 99 percent of the time. (That's a lot of wasteful waiting!) And frankly, waiting on the *wrong* things just makes me *so very weary.*

God expects me to wait for *Him "more"* than all these other things that *so* consume me. After all, He's promised He will *accomplish what concerns me* as I wait on Him (Psalm 138:3, 8). And He *never* overlooks my requests—though I may get a *no* or *keep waiting.*

I obviously can't spend the most hours of my day on my knees waiting on God, **but *my most earnest, heart- and mind-invested waiting* needs to be on *Him.*** This is the *tough* part and *essential* part of what He wants to do in and through me.

Waiting for where God wants to shine *new light* each day is what will give me *life* and *"hope."* Precious hope! Plus it greatly affects the *hows* and *whys* of the *rest* of my waiting! And as I release all the other things that *so* easily consume my waiting thoughts into His hands, I find *peace, satisfaction,* and *thankfulness.* I need to place all of who God is *between* me and all of my other waiting thoughts.

> *"My soul, wait in silence for God only, For my hope is from Him" (Psalm 62:5).*

And of course, waiting for God will make my *worship* sweeter as He envelopes me in His *new light* for the day and opens my eyes to greater wonders of *who He is* there.

Lord God, help us to wait on You "more than the watchmen for the morning. Indeed, more than the watchmen for the morning."

Reflect

What do I spend too much time waiting for? What consumes my most earnest heart- and mind-invested waiting? What steps should I take to make sure I wait for God more than all these other things? How should I allow waiting on God to influence my worship life?

Respond

My God, thank You for the new light You shine into my life each day. I praise You for the hope Your Word brings into my life. And I praise You for the peace and satisfaction I gain in waiting on You. Show me when my heart and mind are more consumed with waiting on other things than I wait on You. And teach me to wait for You above all else. . . . <continue>

DAY FORTY-FOUR
But

Confession: The battle to not focus on *me* seems never-ending. I hate it. By *me*, I mean that constant pull to focus on my feelings, my inadequacies, my insecurities, my needs—who I am, who I'm not, what I have, and what I don't have. That spiritual battle rages supreme.

So worship is that place for me where I can *reset* my sights. It's that place where God fills my space and helps me to cast off the sin, lies, and distortions so I can remember *who He is* in the midst of them.

These "But God. . ." moments are my favorite. They're healing. Restoring. Refreshing. Energizing. And confirming. *When* I bow my heart and mind to the God who is revealing Himself to me.

There are so many great "But God" moments in the Bible. Take Ephesians 2 for example:

> *"And you were dead in your trespasses and sins, . . . [followed by more about those sins] . . .* **But God***, being rich in mercy, because of His great love with which He loved us, even when we were dead in our transgressions, made us alive together with Christ (by grace you have been saved) . . . (vv. 1, 4).*

Here's more:

> "Lord, how many are my foes! How many rise up against me! Many are saying of me, 'God will not deliver him.' **But you, Lord,** are a shield around me, my glory, the One who lifts my head high. I call out to the Lord, and he answers me from his holy mountain" (Psalm 3:1-4, NIV).

I thank God that I don't have the enemies David had! But the strength and peace he found in his "But God" moments teach us a lot about the power of switching our focus from *me* to *Thee*.

Even Jonah had a "But God" moment while in the belly of the fish:

> "I said, 'I have been banished from your sight; yet I will look again toward your holy temple.' The engulfing waters threatened me, the deep surrounded me; seaweed was wrapped around my head. To the roots of the mountains I sank down; the earth beneath barred me in forever. **But You, Lord my God**, brought my life up from the pit. When my life was ebbing away, I remembered you, Lord, and my prayer rose to you, to your holy temple" (Jonah 2:4-7, NIV).

And one of my favorites:

> "My flesh and my heart may fail, **But God** is the strength of my heart and my portion forever" (Psalm 73:26).

Seeking and Savoring

There is so much power in "But God" moments. *And* in "But God" worship. *Satan can't fight the truth of who God is!* So when we struggle to bow our hearts and minds in worship because all we see is all that's around *me*, start the next sentence with, "But God."

> I am weak. → **But God**, You are strong (Psalm 62:7).
>
> I am tired. → **But God**, You never grow weary or tired (Isaiah 40:28).
>
> I am burdened. → **But God**, You carry my load and give me rest (Matthew 11:28).
>
> I am inadequate. → **But God**, through You I can do all things (Philippians 4:13).
>
> I am lonely. → **But God**, You are always with me (Psalm 73:23).
>
> I am afraid. → **But God**, You are my refuge (Psalm 94:22).
>
> I am sick. → **But God**, You are my healer (Exodus 15:26).
>
> I am a sinner (self-centered, unloving, judgmental, lazy . . .) → **But God**, You are my forgiver and my redeemer (1 John 1:9).

I could go on and on and on. Right?

But

Bow your focus and your heart to worship *that* God. Bow to the One who is far greater that anything you can throw His way. The One who has overcome the world! Give *Him* the glory! Know His Word so you can claim its truth about your God — and about *who you are in Him*!

Make "But God" part of your worship so you can put your focus on the One who deserves it completely. And then enjoy the peace and victory that comes from submitting and responding in worship to your mighty God!

Reflect

Which "But God" promise(s) do I need to embrace most right now? (For more guidance, look at the Names of God appendix.) Which area of my life do I find it hardest to take my focus off of me to put it on who God is for me in that place? What steps do I need to take to make "But God" a part of my personal worship life? What victory do I look forward to as a result?

Seeking and Savoring

Respond

Lord God, thank You that You are far greater than anything this life can throw my way. I praise You for overcoming the world! Teach me to bow my focus and heart to who I know You to be so you can replace my displaced thoughts and feelings with Your truth. I praise You for the peace and victory that comes from submitting to you in worship. . . . <continue>

DAY FORTY-FIVE
Reverence

Ever think about *how* we should approach God in worship? I'm not talking about where we worship, the position of our bodies, or even the words we use—but more our *attitude* before Him. I ask, because I've been grappling with these verses:

> "But as for me, by Your abundant lovingkindness I will enter Your house, At Your holy temple I will **bow in reverence** for You" (Psalm 5:7).

> "**Worship the** Lord **with reverence** And rejoice with trembling" (Psalm 2:11).

> "You shall keep My sabbaths and **reverence My sanctuary; I am the** Lord" (Leviticus 26:2).

> "Then the Lord said, 'Because this people draw near with their words And honor Me with their lip service, But they remove their **hearts** far from Me, And their **reverence** for Me consists of tradition learned by rote' " (Isaiah 29:13).

> "Therefore let us be grateful for receiving a kingdom that cannot be shaken, and thus let us **offer to God acceptable worship, with reverence and awe**" (Hebrews 12:28, ESV).

God not only calls us to *worship* Him, but to worship Him with *reverence* and *awe*. Because that's the kind of worship our God Most High finds *"acceptable."*

Friends, are we guilty of ignoring *reverence*? Or dismissing it altogether? In today's church, do we grasp reverence *at all*?

As these verses have turned over and over in my mind, I've had the sinking feeling we approach God *far* too casually or half-heartedly much of the time. It's as if He *weren't really there* or didn't *deserve* more than we throw His way without much thought or preparation. (For comparison, picture how our worship might change if the invisible God became *visible* before us!)

According to the Isaiah verse, **reverence** does *not* result from using just the right *"words"* or engaging in *"tradition learned by rote."* But he says it's a *"heart"* issue.

It's the heart obeying His command to keep the *"Sabbath"* reverent in worship. It's the heart responding in humility to His *"abundant lovingkindness"* that even *allows* us to *"bow"* before Him. And most of all, it's the heart acknowledging *who our God is*, remembering *what He's done* for us, and responding in unmitigated *"grateful"ness* and *"awe,"* because . . .

"I am the Lord.*"*

What kind of heart bows in reverence before God? Usually the heart that's already been *still* before Him. It's the heart that's yearned to *see* Him and *know* Him. It's the heart that's *repentant* in the revealing light of

Reverence

His *holiness*. And it's the heart that's overwhelmed by the utter incomprehensibleness that *is* our Lord God Almighty.

So reverence isn't something that's easily whipped up in a moment's notice on Sunday morning over a God we've ignored the rest of the week. The fruit of neglect will be pseudo worship with *"hearts far from Me."*

Not *reverence*. Not *awe*. Not *true worship*.

God deserves nothing less than eyes open upward and hearts *prepared* and *positioned* to bow low in *reverential awe* before our King—whether on Sunday or any other day. (And yes, I long for churches to embrace bowing the knee—the ultimate sign of surrender and reverence. For the Bible also calls for this!) Let's strive for it. Let's *fight* for it. For *He alone is worthy!*

> *"Ascribe to the* Lord *the glory due his name; bring an offering, and come into his courts! Worship the* Lord *in the splendor of holiness; tremble before him, all the earth!" (Psalm 96:8-9, ESV).*

Reflect

How do I think my worship would change if the invisible God became visible before me? What does reverence mean to me? What steps can I take to make sure I'm entering my personal time of worship with more reverence toward God and less casually? How about corporately on Sundays?

Respond

Lord God, I praise You that You are a holy God. And I thank You that despite Your holiness, out of Your incredible love, You still invite me into Your presence. Teach me to worship You with reverence and awe. Show me when I take Your presence too casually instead of having a heart that's seeking after You. Help me to have a heart and mind prepared and positioned to worship You each day. . . . <continue>

DAY FORTY-SIX
Expect

If worship is always the same experience over and over again, then is my focus on the *unsearchable, unfathomable* God? Or is it on a comfortable routine? Is it on inviting God's Spirit to *move* and *reveal*? Or is it on making sure *I'm* still in control somehow?

Would we say *"no"* to God if He sat us down to tell us in advance what He longed for our worship to be? But wait—He has. And sadly, we often do say, "no." Is it fear? Pride? Disinterest? Distractions? Or even distaste?

Either way, sin (or *"whatever is not from faith,"* Romans 14:23) is preventing us from *seeking* and *savoring* our God. And from *welcoming* and *worshiping* Him.

If God is who He says He is—*and He is*—then we need to *trust Him* with our worship *of* Him. We need to let *Him* set the heights and depths. We need to let go of our preconceived ideas and lean into *His* purpose and intimacy in worship with *great expectation* and *awe*.

He gave us His Holy Spirit for moments such as these. (Okay, and for every other moment.) His Spirit guides, enlightens, encourages, reveals, convicts, and prepares us for the foot of the throne. *There is no substitute.*

Seeking and Savoring

And then we need to *expect God to be God*.

Expect (among other things):

1) His promised presence – "... the LORD is with you when you are with Him. And if you seek Him, He will let you find Him" *(2 Chronicles 15:2).*

2) His revealed glory – *"Thus I have seen You in the sanctuary, To see Your power and Your glory"* (Psalm 63:2).

3) Convicted sin – *"Holy, Holy, Holy, is the LORD of hosts ... Woe is me, for I am ruined! ... For my eyes have seen the King, the LORD of hosts"* (Isaiah 6:3,5).

4) Changed perspective, with moments of – *"Until I came into the sanctuary of God; then I perceived their end"* (Psalm 73:17).

5) Spiritual transformation – *"And we, who with unveiled faces all reflect the glory of the Lord, are being transformed into his image with intensifying glory, which comes from the Lord, who is the Spirit"* (2 Corinthians 3:18, BSB).

The more you entrust to God — to your *unfathomable* God (so *know* Him) — the freer He is to work and move to *draw* you into a time of purer, deeper, personal worship. What an incredible picture of who He is — of His incredible love for us and His amazing grace towards us!

So ask God what *His* desire is for your worship — what you need to open your hands to and what you need to let go of (especially sin). How does He want you to prepare for worship, and what does He want you to *offer* Him

Expect

when you come? Don't rush His answer—*listen*. And invite *Him* to set the heights and depths of your times at His feet as He opens your eyes to His glory. Then refuse to settle for the same routine over and over. *Expect God to be God* when you worship!

Reflect

What do I feel is the greatest inhibitor to allowing God control of my worship of Him? What do I expect when I come to worship? Am I confident in what I offer Him when I worship? How do I feel He's leading me to grow in this respect?

Respond

Heavenly Father, I thank and praise You for Your indwelling Holy Spirit who prepares and guides me for worship. I praise You for Your incredible love and amazing grace that continually draws me deeper still. Teach me what Your desire is for my worship. Show me what I need to let go of or offer You that I still cling to. I invite You to set the heights and depths of my times with You and open my eyes to Your glory. . . . <continue>

DAY FORTY-SEVEN
Conversation

Are you in an ongoing, nonstop conversation with God? I mean, the kind where you attentively listen and are quick to reply?

I think that's the idea behind the command to *"pray without ceasing" (1 Thessalonians 5:17) — acknowledging* God's presence throughout the day, *including* Him in our decisions, *thanking* Him for His help, *looking* to Him for guidance, and then stopping to *respond* to His *goodness, grace,* and *glory* with *worship.*

As we carefully listen to God's voice throughout the day, we hear Him say things like:

"Follow Me" (Luke 9:23).

"Draw near to listen" (Ecclesiastes 5:1).

"Don't fear" (Luke 5:10).

"What do you want Me to do for you?" (Mark 10:51).

"Be strong and courageous" (Joshua 1:9).

"Come to Me" (Matthew 11:28).

Conversation

"Be still, and know I am God" (Psalm 46:10, ESV).

"Have faith in God" (Mark 11:22).

"I love you" (John 17:23, paraphrased).

When our hearts are inclined to hear His gentle words — *drawing* and *encouraging*, *reminding* and *comforting*, *rebuking* and *loving* us — they fan the flames of our worship. Because there's nothing more *beautiful* than His voice and His face. Nothing more *powerful*. Nothing more *unspeakably awesome* and *holy*.

Correction: Nothing more *"holy, holy, holy"* (Revelation 4:8)!

If you're struggling to worship throughout the week — struggling to *want* to worship — focus on nurturing your *ongoing* conversation with God. And don't neglect to surrender to His voice *calling* you and *pleading* with you to *come* to the quiet place — the *"secret place"* (Psalm 91:1, NKJV) — to commune with Him.

Don't hear Him? Lean in *further*. Wait *longer*. Respond to the prompts to confess sin. *Surrender all*.

And then do it *again*.

You see, we can't out-seek God! We can't wear out His desire to be *with* us, His eagerness to *encourage* us, or His passion to *share Himself* with us.

And then **respond in complete surrender with everything you are to all of the God who is passionately revealing**

Seeking and Savoring

Himself to you. That's the *worship* part of the conversation. The *most important* part of the conversation—and our calling as believers in Jesus (Philippians 2:9-11).

He's always waiting and *longing* for your heart to commune with His. And He joyfully receives any *humble offering of worship* you have to pour out. He *loves* it when He reveals, "Here's who I am," and we *respond* with, "I believe! I worship You!"

Engage in the *listening*—and then in the *responding*. Let your conversation with God usher you into worship. Every day. Do you hear Him?

Reflect

Do I struggle to be in an ongoing conversation with God? Do I struggle to lean in to hear His voice? How do I sense Him leading me to respond to His invitation to commune with Him more? How should I use that to fuel my worship?

Respond

Lord God, I thank and praise You that I don't have to doubt Your constant presence or Your desire to be in constant communication with me. That's beyond my comprehension! Teach me to seek You. Give me ears attentive to Your voice and a heart quick to respond. Nudge me when

Conversation

I'm not listening to Your attempts to commune with me. And help me to have a surrendered heart. . . . <continue>

DAY FORTY-EIGHT
Broken

It would be hard to beat the powerful effect of *brokenness* on our worship — those moments when we see ourselves in light of who Jesus is and bow in humble response.

It's all too common for Christians to quickly brush off sin. We say a short prayer asking for forgiveness, but don't often enough take the time to grasp the impact of our sin on our relationship with God *or* to comprehend His willingness and power to forgive it.

A particular Pharisee invited Jesus to his house for dinner (Luke 7:36-50) when an unexpected — or even *unwelcomed* — guest arrived. But this guest didn't come for the food. She heard Jesus was there, and her brokenness compelled her to track Him down and empty herself at His feet. That's where her contrite heart soaked in His amazing mercy as she wiped His tear-covered feet with her hair — kissing and anointing them with perfume.

The Pharisee's thoughts of this woman weren't surprising: *"If this man were a prophet He would know who and what sort of person this woman is who is touching Him, that she is a sinner"* (v. 39).

And Jesus *answered* the Pharisee's thoughts with a parable about how someone forgiven a large debt will love the forgiver *more* than he who had been forgiven *little*. Then . . .

> "Turning toward the woman, He said to Simon, 'Do you see this woman? I entered your house; you gave Me no water for My feet, but she has wet My feet with her tears and wiped them with her hair. You gave Me no kiss; but she, since the time I came in, has not ceased to kiss My feet. You did not anoint My head with oil, but she anointed My feet with perfume. For this reason I say to you, her sins, which are many, have been forgiven, for [that is why] she loved much; but he who is forgiven little, loves little.' Then He said to her, 'Your sins have been forgiven' " (Luke 7:44, 48).

The Pharisee failed to recognize who Jesus was. He didn't see His *holiness*, His *power*, His *truth*, or His *love*. Instead He *misunderstood* and *underestimated* his dinner guest. He didn't even offer Him the courtesy He owed a *common* guest in his own home. Much less respond to *who Jesus truly was*.

In contrast, this despised woman gave from the very depths of her broken soul to the Man she recognized as *worthy*. Her kisses weren't just lip service in hopes of being let off the hook for her sin. The Greek words show that she kissed Him *profusely* and her tears fell *uncontrollably*. And seeing her faith (v. 50) and brokenness, He *forgave* her.

Whether we're guilty of the immorality of this woman or something much less repulsive in our own eyes, the truth is, *it's a debt none of us can afford to pay*. It's a debt

Seeking and Savoring

that requires our place at His feet where our brokenness gives way to His *mercy* and *holiness* in humble repentance. And whether our expression to our Forgiver comes in the form of uncontrollable tears or quiet whispers, He *knows* and *responds* to the intent of our *hearts*.

And here's the real kicker: *This woman didn't know that Jesus was about to die for her sins.* She didn't yet understand the *price* that He was willing to pay for the actions that separated her from God and repulsed the Pharisee.

But we do.

How much *more* should our hearts respond in brokenness when we see our stains, great or small, in the light of His *incomprehensible sacrifice* and *mercy? How much more?*

It's *indescribable. Incalculable.* The debt we owe is *so much greater* than what this woman could've possibly conceived! And *that* should drive us to His nail-scarred feet in unbridled worship.

Ask to see His *glory*. Strive to grasp His *holiness* and *mercy*. And *respond*.

Reflect

How does the story of this broken woman's worship affect me? Do I think brokenness is something that's

Broken

often missing in our worship—or in my worship? How do I feel God is calling me to respond to Him out of my place(s) of brokenness?

Respond

Oh, heavenly Father, the depths of Your love, and mercy, and grace are beyond what I can fathom. Thank You for welcoming me to Your feet in my brokenness. I praise You for paying the debt that I owed so I could come into Your presence to worship You. May my heart conceive of the grief You feel when I allow sin to separate our fellowship together. Teach me to have a heart that won't settle for less than You. . . . <continue>

DAY FORTY-NINE
Cost

Did you know our worship of God should *cost* us something? Yes, I know Jesus paid the ultimate price for our sins once and for all time so we might spend eternity with Him. But when it comes to our *worship* of God, the Bible often talks about it as our *"sacrifice."*

Consider these verses:

> *"Through Him then, let us continually offer up a **sacrifice of praise** to God, that is, the fruit of lips that give thanks to His name"* (Hebrews 13:15).

> *"Therefore I urge you, brethren, by the mercies of God, to present your bodies a living and **holy sacrifice, acceptable to God**, which is your **spiritual service of worship**"* (Romans 12:1).

In Old Testament times, God set aside festivals at various times of the year for believers to journey to the temple to make their sacrifices. It was a time of setting aside the routines and obligations of life to focus on and celebrate their relationship with Him. It was a time of surrender as well as action.

But now, *we* are *each* the temple (1 Corinthians 6:19)! So we don't have to make a long journey to worship our

God. He's always here! Always waiting. But that doesn't mean we shouldn't *still* make the sacrifice of time, attention, and focus—giving God all He deserves during that time we set aside to worship Him.

I'm challenged by David's words in 2 Samuel 24:18-24. The prophet Gad told David to erect an altar to the Lord with the specifics that he should get the threshing floor from Araunah the Jebusite. When David told Araunah the threshing floor was for building an altar to God (so He'd hold back the plague from the Israelites), Araunah made the offer for David to take the flooring at no expense. How generous! But David replied, *"No, but I will surely buy it from you for a price, for **I will not offer burnt offerings to the Lord my God which cost me nothing.**"* And the Lord was moved by David's prayer for the land at that altar and held back the plague.

Also challenging is a word from the prophet Malachi (1:7-13) to the priests in Israel:

> *" 'Oh that there were one among you who would shut the gates, that you might not **uselessly kindle fire on My altar**! I am not pleased with you,' says the Lord of hosts, 'nor will I accept an offering from you. . . . You also say, "My, how tiresome it is!" And you disdainfully sniff at it,' says the Lord of hosts, 'and you bring what was taken by robbery and what is lame or sick; so you bring the offering! Should I receive that from your hand?' says the Lord" (vv. 10, 13).*

In other words, in no way should our worship be a careless, thoughtless act, but instead, a *response* of *complete surrender* of all we are and have—an offering worthy of

Seeking and Savoring

God's acceptance. Otherwise, we're *"uselessly kindling fire"* on His altar. Our attitudes matter. He knows when we find worship *"tiresome,"* and He won't receive it. He also knows where the spiritual battle lies with each of us, and His Holy Spirit will faithfully guide the way!

Because our Jesus? He is perfect, holy, and changeless. And as we focus on who He is, what He has done, and is doing, and promises to do, then *"through Him"* we need to *"continually offer up a sacrifice of praise."*

And what's the *"sacrifice"* — the *"cost?"* It's *"thankful"* and surrendered hearts. It's *"holy"* and *"acceptable"* offerings (pure — no unconfessed sin). And it's time and attention spent focusing on Jesus, and the determination to love the Lord our God with all our heart, soul, and mind (Luke 10:27). Lest we also say, *"How tiresome it is!"* in our times worshiping Him. None of us want to hear God's heartbreaking reply, *"I am not pleased with you."*

Ask God often what He wants you to offer to Him in worship. Don't rush it. Follow His Spirit's leading. Listen. And obey. The cost of offering our God what He deserves and requires in worship is the greatest privilege on this earth! And one that reaps extravagant joy.

Cost

Reflect

Have I ever considered the cost or sacrifice of my worship? Where do my spiritual battles lie when it comes to worship? Do I feel like my worship is acceptable to God? What steps can I take to assure my worship looks the way He desires it to look?

Respond

Lord God, I thank You that You are perfect, holy, and changeless. Thank You for being the only god worthy of all the time and attention I could ever offer You. May You find my heart pure and my worship acceptable every day. Help me to seek You regularly and allow Your Spirit to usher me to Your throne. . . . <continue>

DAY FIFTY
Shadrach (et al)

I've learned from personal experience the importance of being prepared to fight distractions *from* worship and idols clamoring *for* my worship. And these disturbances come in all shapes, sizes, and personalities. That's because the enemy will do *anything* to stop us from worshiping the One True God. He can't stop us from *believing* in God, but if he can distract us from *bowing* to Him, that's a victory he greatly enjoys.

The bar is set quite high when it comes to not caving to idols or distractions from worship. If anyone could've qualified for a "grace pass," it would've been Shadrach, Meshach, and Abednego.

In case you don't remember how this all got started, Nebuchadnezzar, king of Babylon, took over Judah and demanded that everyone bow to his golden statue or face certain death (Daniel 3:1-30)! And Shadrach, Meshach, and Abednego *refused.* So, . . .

> "Nebuchadnezzar . . . said to them, 'Is it true, Shadrach, Meshach and Abednego, that you do not serve my gods or worship the golden image that I have set up? . . . if you do not worship [it], you will immediately be cast into the midst of a furnace of blazing fire; and what god is there who can deliver

you out of my hands?' Shadrach, Meshach and Abednego replied to the king, 'O Nebuchadnezzar, we do not need to give you an answer concerning this matter. If it be so, **our God whom we serve is able to deliver us from the furnace of blazing fire; and He will deliver us out of your hand, O king. But even if He does not, let it be known to you, O king, that we are not going to serve your gods or worship the golden image that you have set up'** " (Daniel 3:14-18, emphasis mine).

Not only did the now-famous trio not cave to the king's threatening command to bow to his idol, but they also responded with absolutely *no* hesitation or fear. *How* could they do that? They *knew their God!* Yes, they knew God had saved them from one of Nebuchadnezzar's previous threats (Daniel 2:17-49). But most of all, the God they loved and worshiped was the *very same worthy God regardless of whether He saved them or not!*

Of course, we all know how this dramatic story ends. An infuriated Nebuchadnezzar heats the furnace seven times hotter than usual, and ties up and tosses in the three friends (with the heat killing the men who throw them in). Then God not only saves Shadrach, Meshach, and Abednego, but they are also joined by a fourth man *"with the appearance like a son of the gods"(v. 25),* and all were completely untouched and unharmed by the flames.

Then Nebuchadnezzar responds by decreeing that no one speak against the Most High God of these men! *"Blessed be the God of Shadrach, Meshach, and Abednego"* (*v. 28*)! I believe *this* was God's greater goal — *the powerful glory brought to His name as a result!*

Thankfully, the things that threaten our worship loyalty don't remotely resemble an evil king or a fiery furnace. (*Pray* for those whose does!) And our potential idols don't come right out and say, "I'm trying to distract you from worshiping God!"

So the main thing? Like Shadrach, Meshach, and Abednego, we need to *never stop growing to know and love God more*. The closer we are to *Jesus*, the more prepared we'll be for unexpected moments of pressure to declare without wavering, *This is who my God is, and I will not bow to you instead. I will not give you the time, attention, loyalty, or piece of my heart that God alone deserves.*

We must be on the alert to recognize the endless, well-disguised idols that are clamoring for our *misplaced attention* and *bowed knee*. *Good things* and *bad. Important* and *worthless. In church* and *out.* Satan has a knack for knowing what will distract each of us from God's throne. We need to know the biblical truths to combat them, and pray for the *wisdom, determination,* and *courage* to say, "*no!*"

And considering Shadrach, Meshach, and Abednego further, it helps to have close friends with the same convictions to stand side by side and encourage one another in their faithfulness to God. (It's easier to not have to face those furnaces alone!)

Now, the best news?

God's love never stops *drawing* us and *compelling* us. His *patience* and *grace* extend way into our *seeking* of Him and our *worship* of Him. He longs for us to lift our eyes *off* of ourselves and all the distractions and fix our eyes and heart on *Him*. That's where the *passion* and *strength* to remain a loyal worshiper come from.

> *"My heart is fixed, O God, my heart is fixed: I will sing and give praise" (Psalm 57:7, KJV)!*

And the response of those close enough to observe your victory? "Blessed be the God of <*your name*>!"

God's glory!

Reflect
What are the potential idols clamoring for my loyalty right now? Do I feel prepared for unexpected moments of pressure to declare my loyalty to God? What steps should I take to ensure my eyes and heart are set on worshiping Him alone?

Seeking and Savoring

Respond

Lord God, thank You that Your love never stops compelling me to draw near to You. I praise You for Your patience and grace that always meet me here. Help me to never stop striving to know and love You more. Help me to recognize idols that are clamoring for my attention and bowed knee. Give me courage and determination to say "no" to them. May my heart always be fixed on You. . . .
<continue>

*This devotion includes excerpts from my book, *Worship and the Word*.

DAY FIFTY-ONE
Listen

It was one of those moments when God led me somewhere in His Word I didn't set out to go so I'd read something I needed to hear.

The concept of stopping to listen to God isn't new to me. It's something I do regularly—though it's frequently a battle. But these verses I'd read many times before struck me in a new and profound way this time.

> *"Guard your steps when you go to the house of God.* **Go near to listen** *rather than to offer the sacrifice of fools, who do not know that they do wrong.* **Do not be quick** *with your mouth,* **do not be hasty** *in your heart to utter anything before God. God is in heaven and you are on earth, so let your words be few"* (Ecclesiastes 5:1-2, NIV, emphasis mine).

I stopped and grabbed my journal and wrote:

I need to listen MORE and I need to listen FIRST.

How would it change my prayer life and *worship* life if I listened to God *"when [I] go"—first—*before speaking—lest I *"offer the sacrifice of fools"*?

Seeking and Savoring

Sure, I know I need to have a heart prepared—seeking, humbled, and repentant—to worship God. And I always ask the Holy Spirit to guide my worship—help me fight distractions and focus on Him alone. But what if I need to *"go near to listen" first*, so I'm not too *"quick"* or *"hasty"* (or the NASB says, *"impulsive"*) in what I *"utter"* to Him? (*Me? Impulsive?*)

I'm already careful about how I enter worship, but this made my worship-loving mouth fall open.

What if stopping—*really stopping*—to ask my God, *"What do You want me to know? What do You want from me today?"* made my worship more pure . . . intimate . . . or *beautiful* to Him?

- Maybe He wants to *"guard my steps"* as I enter worship—help me slow down and focus on Him so I can better fight distractions or move beyond the tradition.
- Maybe He wants me to give the Holy Spirit space to reveal an unnoticed sin.
- Maybe He wants me to surrender something to Him that I'm clinging too tightly to that might keep me from surrendering to *Him*.
- Or perhaps He wants to remind me of His unfailing love, new mercies, or resurrection power as I enter my time at His feet.

I obviously can't outguess what God might want to do with that time, only that He's requested it—so I need to do it. That's all I need to know. Plus, *it's inviting the promised work of His Holy Spirit within us!*

Listen

"*But the Helper, the Holy Spirit, whom the Father will send in My name, He will teach you all things, and bring to your remembrance all that I said to you*" (*John 14:26*).

That doesn't mean I don't need to listen for Him *during* worship. Just that I need to remember to *begin* my time by *inviting whatever He has for me there.*

So whether I'm entering a time of worship at home or church,

> **I need to listen MORE and I need to listen FIRST.**

"*. . . the* LORD *is with you when you are with Him. And if you seek Him, He will let you find Him*" (*2 Chronicles 15:2*).

Reflect

Is the idea of listening to God unfamiliar or uncomfortable for me? What questions do I feel God is leading me to ask Him before I approach Him in worship? How do I see the concept of "listen MORE and listen FIRST" impacting my worship life?

Seeking and Savoring

Respond

God, I praise You once again for Your love that invites and allows me into Your presence. I thank You for the intimacy that You long for that guides my time and worship of You. May I be obedient to stop and listen for You. Increase my longing and ability to hear Your voice so I might be better prepared to offer You what You deserve and desire from me in worship. . . . <continue>

DAY FIFTY-TWO
Him

As we approach God's throne in worship, the bottom line is always—*make it about Him.*

What if I don't like the songs? Make it about *Him.*

What if I'm too distracted? Make it about *Him.*

What if I've had a tough week? Make it about *Him.*

What if I just don't feel like it? Make it about *Him.*

Whatever *"what if . . ."* statement I'm dwelling on in that moment, it frankly doesn't matter. Because it's not about *me.* It's about surrendering each of those flailing thoughts and feelings at the feet of the *One* who deserves our absolute *all.* It's about realizing that *He* is God and I'm *not.* It's about rebuking the enemy's attempts at stealing our attention away from worshiping our holy God. It's about allowing Him to rein in our focus to put it where it's most deserved. And it's about trusting Him to move in and through us to offer back to Him all He's given us to begin with. It's *only, ever about Him.*

Because if it's not solely about God, it's not worship *of* God. The lies are potent! They rob God of the worship

He deserves and they rob us of the intimacy and transforming power we can only find at His feet.

So fight the battle before you go. Fill your mind with truth.

Replace the complaints with thanksgiving to God. "***Enter His gates with thanksgiving*** *and* [then] *His courts with praise*" *(Psalm 100:4).*

Replace the distraction of the week with prayers asking God to empower your worship. "***My heart is fixed****, O God, my heart is fixed: I will sing and give praise*" *(Psalm 57:7, KJV)!*

Replace the distance you're feeling from God with words surrendered to whatever He wants for you in that place. "***Be still, and know*** *that I am God.* ***I will be exalted*** *among the nations, I will be exalted in the earth!*" *(Psalm 46:10, ESV).*

Replace the lies about worship or God with the truth of His Word. "*O send out* ***Your light and Your truth*** *(His Word),* ***let them lead me; Let them bring me to Your holy hill*** *(the place for worship) . . . Then I will go to the altar of God, To God my exceeding joy; And upon the lyre* ***I shall praise You****, O God, my God*" *(Psalm 43:3-4).*

Replace sin with repentance and His cleansing forgiveness. "*Therefore, brethren, since we have confidence to enter the holy place* [the place for worship] *by the blood of Jesus, let us* ***draw near with a sincere heart*** *in full assurance of faith, having our* ***hearts sprinkled clean*** *from an evil* *conscience and our bodies washed with pure water" (Hebrews 10:19, 22).*

Replace your doubts about God's presence with the promise He is near: *"Draw near to God and **He will draw near to you**" (James 4:8a).*

Our great God rewards any attempt at approaching Him with glimpses of His goodness and glory. We can't out-search God! And every glimpse of His greatness adds to our infinite reasons to worship Him every day!

And what about those "what if" pains, concerns, or distractions? He cares about those too. So as you make that moment about *Him*, offer *those* to Him to do with as He wills— inviting Him to move in, through, and around you for His ultimate glory.

So come (whether at home or church) prepared and determined to make it *all about Him*. Ask God what you need to know as you prepare to worship Him. Ask His Spirit to guide and empower your worship. These are prayers He would love to answer!

> *"I, by Your great love, can come into Your house; in reverence I bow down toward Your holy temple" (Psalm 5:7, NIV).*

Seeking and Savoring

Reflect

What are my most common "what if . . ." statements when worship is a struggle? What lies or distractions does the enemy throw my way to interfere with my worship? What truths from God's Word do I need to embrace most to combat those lies or distractions? What should I do to be more prepared to make it about God for my times of worshiping Him?

Respond

Lord God, thank You that Your truth is more real and powerful than anything else in my life. I praise You that when I come to worship, I come to worship the One True God, God my Redeemer, God my Rock, God my Fortress, and God my Strength. Help me to make it all about You alone. Help me to take my eyes off of myself and the things around me so I can give You all the glory You deserve. And help me to remember Your Word to counteract the distractions and lies. You alone are God, and there is none like You. . . . <continue>

APPENDIX
Names, Titles, and Descriptions of God

Father

A faithful God who does no wrong
A forgiving God
A fortress of salvation
A glorious crown
A jealous and avenging God
A Master in heaven
A refuge for His people
A refuge for the needy in His distress
A refuge for the oppressed
A refuge for the poor
A sanctuary
A shade from the heat
A shelter from the storm
A source of strength
A stronghold in times of trouble
An ever-present help in trouble
Architect and builder
Builder of everything
Commander of the Lord's army
Creator of heaven and earth
Defender of widows
Eternal King
Father
Father of compassion
Father of our spirits
Father of the heavenly lights
Father to the fatherless
God **(El)**
God Almighty **(El Shaddai)**
God and Father of our Lord Jesus Christ

Seeking and Savoring

God Most High **(El Elyon)**
God my Maker
God my Rock
God my Savior
God my Stronghold
God of Abraham, Isaac, and Jacob
God of all comfort
God of all mankind
God of glory
God of grace
God of hope
God of love and peace
God of peace
God of retribution
God of the living
God of the spirits of all mankind
God of truth
God Our Father
God Our Strength
God over all the kingdoms of the earth
God the Father
God with Us **(Immanuel)**
God who avenges me
God who gives endurance and encouragement
God who relents from sending calamity
God Who Sees **(El Roi)**
Great and awesome God
Great and powerful God
Great, mighty, and awesome God
He who blots out your transgressions
He who comforts you
He who forms the hearts of all
He who raised Christ from the dead
He who reveals His thoughts to man
Helper of the fatherless
Him who is able to do immeasurably more than all we ask or imagine
Him who is able to keep you from falling
Him who is ready to judge the living and the dead
Holy Father
Holy One
Holy One among you
I AM **(Hayah)**
I AM WHO I AM **(Hayah Asher Hayah)**
Jealous **(Qanna)**
Judge of all the earth
King of Glory
King of Heaven
Living and True God
Lord, Master **(Adonai)**
Lord Almighty

Names, Titles, and Descriptions of God

- Lord God Almighty
- Lord Is Peace **(Jehovah Shalom)**
- Lord **(Yahweh, Jehovah)**
- Lord Most High
- Lord My Banner **(Jehovah Nissi)**
- Lord My Rock
- Lord of All the Earth
- Lord of Heaven and Earth
- Lord of Kings
- Lord of Hosts/Powers **(Jehovah Sabaoth)**
- Lord Our God
- Lord Our Maker
- Lord Our Righteousness **(Jehovah Tsidkenu)**
- Lord Our Shepherd **(Jehovah Rohi)**
- Lord Our Shield
- Lord Who Heals **(Jehovah Rapha)**
- Lord Who Is There **(Jehovah Shammah)**
- Lord Who Makes You Holy **(Jehovah Mekoddishkem)**
- Lord Who Strikes the Blow
- Lord Will Provide **(Jehovah Jireh)**
- Love
- Maker of all things
- Maker of heaven and earth
- Most High
- My Advocate
- My Comforter in sorrow
- My Confidence
- My Help
- My Helper
- My Hiding Place
- My Hope
- My Light
- My Mighty Rock
- My Refuge in the day of disaster
- My Refuge in times of trouble
- My Song
- My Strong Deliverer
- Only wise God
- Our Dwelling Place
- Our Judge
- Our Lawgiver
- Our Leader
- Our Mighty One
- Our Redeemer
- Our Refuge and Strength
- Righteous Father
- Righteous Judge
- Rock of our salvation
- Shepherd
- Sovereign Lord
- The Almighty
- The compassionate and gracious God

Seeking and Savoring

The Eternal God
The consuming fire
The Everlasting God **(El Olam)**
The exalted God
The faithful God
The Gardener (husbandman)
The glorious Father
The Glory of Israel
The God of the Covenant **(El Berith)**
The God who saves me
The God who sees me
The Great King above all gods
The Just and Mighty One
The Living Father
The Majestic Glory
The Majesty in heaven
The One who sustains me
The only God
The Potter
The Rock in whom I take refuge
The Spring of Living Water
The strength of my heart
The true God
You who hear prayer
You who judge righteously and test the heart and mind
You who keep your covenant of love with your servants
You who love the people
Your glory
Your praise
Your very great reward

Jesus

A Banner for the Peoples
A Nazarene
All
Alpha and Omega
Ancient of Days
Anointed One
Apostle and High Priest
Author and Perfecter of our faith
Author of Life
Author of their salvation
Blessed and only Ruler
Branch of the Lord
Bread of God
Bread of life
Bridegroom
Chief cornerstone
Christ Jesus my Lord
Christ Jesus our hope
Christ of God
Consolation of Israel
Covenant for the people

Names, Titles, and Descriptions of God

Crown of splendor
Eternal life
Faithful and True
Faithful and true witness
First to rise from the dead
Firstborn from among the dead
Firstborn over all creation
First fruits of those that have fallen asleep
Fragrant offering and sacrifice of God
Friend of tax collectors and sinners
God of all the earth
God over all
God's Son
Great High Priest
Great Light
Great Shepherd of the sheep
Guarantee of a better covenant
He who comes down from heaven and gives life to the world
He who searches hearts and minds
Head of every man
Head of the body, the Church
Head of the Church
Head over every power and authority
Heir of all things
Him who died and came to life again
Him who loves us and has freed us from our sins
His one and only Son
Holy and Righteous One
Holy One of God
Holy servant Jesus
Hope of Israel
Horn of Salvation
Image of the Invisible God
Immanuel (God with us)
Indescribable gift
Jesus
Jesus Christ
Jesus Christ our Lord
Jesus Christ our Savior
Jesus of Nazareth
Judge of the living and the dead
KING OF KINGS
King of the ages
Lamb of God
Light for revelation to the Gentiles
Light of Life
Light of Men
Light of the World
Living Bread that came down from heaven

Lord and Savior Jesus Christ Lord (Kurios)
Lord of Glory
LORD OF LORDS
Lord of Peace
Lord of the Harvest
Lord of the Sabbath
Lord (Rabboni)
Man accredited by God
Man of Sorrows
Master
Mediator of a new covenant
Merciful and faithful High Priest
Messenger of the covenant Messiah
Morning Star
My Friend
My Intercessor
One who makes men holy
One who speaks to the Father in our defense
One who will arise to rule over the nations
Our glorious Lord Jesus Christ
Our God and Savior Jesus Christ
Our only Sovereign and Lord
Our Passover lamb
Our Peace
Our righteousness, holiness, and redemption
Physician
Prince and Savior
Prince of Peace
Prince of Princes
Prince of the Hosts
Ransom for all men
Refiner and purifier
Resurrection and the life
Righteous Judge
Righteous man
Righteous One
Rock Eternal (rock of ages)
Ruler of God's creation
Ruler of the kings of the earth
Savior of the world
Second Man
Shepherd and Overseer of your souls
Son of Man
Son of the Blessed One
Son of the Living God
Son of the Most High God
Source of eternal salvation
Sure Foundation
Teacher
The Amen
The atoning sacrifice for our sins

Names, Titles, and Descriptions of God

The Beginning and the End
The Bright Morning Star
The exact representation of His being
The First and the Last
The Gate (door)
The Good Shepherd
The Head
The Last Adam
The Life
The Living One
The Living Stone
The Lord Our Righteousness
The Man from Heaven
The Man Jesus Christ
The Most Holy
The One and Only
The only God our Savior
The Radiance of God's glory
The Rising of the Sun (Dayspring)
The Stone the builders rejected
The testimony given in its proper time
The True Light
The True Vine
The Truth
The Way
The Word (logos)
True Bread from Heaven
Wisdom from God
Witness to the peoples
Wonderful Counselor
Word of God
Word of life
Your life
Your salvation

Holy Spirit

A deposit (earnest)
Another Counselor
Breath of the Almighty
Holy One
Holy Spirit
Holy Spirit of God
Seal
Spirit of Christ
Spirit of counsel and of power
Spirit of faith
Spirit of fire
Spirit of glory
Spirit of God
Spirit of grace and supplication
Spirit of His Son
Spirit of holiness
Spirit of Jesus Christ
Spirit of judgment
Spirit of justice

Spirit of knowledge and
 of the fear of the Lord
Spirit of life
Spirit of our God
Spirit of the Lord
Spirit of the Sovereign
 Lord
Spirit of truth
Spirit of wisdom and of
 understanding

Spirit of wisdom and
 revelation
The Gift
The promised Holy Spirit
The same gift
Voice of the Almighty
Voice of the Lord

Worship and the Word

Looking for what's next for your personal study, small group, book club, Sunday school, or Bible study? Want to explore what God's Word says about *passionately pursuing* and *intimately engaging* the God of the Bible in worship? Check out Pamela Haddix's book, *Worship and the Word*!

"*Worship and the Word* is an awesome study that oozes with rock solid theology and incredibly practical application. It will challenge you to your core. It will move you from singing songs of the faith to seeking, seeing, knowing, and lifting personally the God of the faith. The insights, studies, and questions have the power to move your heart and mind to authentic worship. Engage the principles Pam shares and you will offer God purer personal worship."

— Dan Webster, Founder
Authentic Leadership, Inc.

You can learn more about *Worship and the Word* at pamelahaddix.com or amazon.com.